THE **A** TO **Z** OF

Wildlife

WATCHING

Introduction

A smooth black fin emerges from the ocean, then another, and two more. Your pulse quickens. It's a family of orcas, resident around the Bay of Islands in New Zealand, and they're hunting rays on the sea floor, clearly visible in these transparent, shallow waters. The fact that this moment, an encounter with such graceful and powerful fellow inhabitants of our planet, was unexpected and unpredictable makes it all the more magical. Such is the joy of watching wildlife in its natural home.

For many people, one of the most rewarding experiences of travel is seeing creatures that you wouldn't encounter back home. Whether you set out to see them deliberately on a safari or spot them through sheer luck, the thrill of watching a wild animal go about its daily business always makes your senses tingle. But, we asked ourselves, how would you know what you had spotted? And if you wanted to see a particular animal, how would you know where to start looking? That was the genesis of this pictorial guide to 300 animals.

To compile this book we turned to the highly experienced biologist and writer Amy-Jane Beer, who created a wishlist of weird and wonderful creatures from around the world. Mark Carwardine, who travels the world photographing wildlife, contributed a foreword. We included all of the most iconic animals – lions, tigers, elephants and sharks – in the alphabetical order but we wanted to go further than those headline acts and showcase much more of the mind-blowing diversity of the natural world. The realisation that such extraordinary wonders have evolved on our planet – these are just 300 out of more than eight million species – is humbling and inevitably prompts questions about our role and place in the world: no matter your age, few things spark curiosity like another living thing.

Between these covers, you'll find descriptions of where to see a multitude of mammals, from snow leopards and mountains goats at the very top of the world, to such resourceful residents of African deserts as antelopes and the fennec fox. In the air, we've got birds and bats, from the giant albatross to thumb-sized hog-nosed bats – and also the occasional gliding lizard, fish or mammal. Under the waves, we'll show you giant clams, corals, whales and the wobbegong. And we could have created a whole book just about incredible insects to spot – from beautiful butterflies to the formidable Hercules beetle. Each entry also suggests some of the places where you will have the best chance of seeing the animal. We hope that this book will inspire you to seek out some of the wildlife you've always wanted to see and add many more creatures to the list.

Amy-Jane Beer

Amy studied Biology at Royal Holloway, University of London, and earned an unglamorous PhD studying the nervous systems of sea urchins. Urchins are fascinating, but with all of nature's myriad splendours out there she found it hard to focus on just one species and set about becoming a generalist, a seeker of wild wonders, and a writer of science and natural history for all ages. She was editor of *Wildlife of Britain* and *Animals Animals Animals* magazines and currently edits *Wildlife World* magazine for the People's Trust for Endangered Species. She writes books, regular features for *BBC Wildlife* magazine and Country Diary columns for *The Guardian*, and is working on her first novel – nature-inspired of course. She helps judge the BTO Bird Photographer of the Year competition. Her favourite wild species? Usually the one she's privileged enough to be looking at.

Mark Carwardine

Mark Carwardine is a zoologist, an outspoken conservationist, a TV and radio presenter, a widely published wildlife photographer, a best-selling author, a wildlife tour operator, a lecturer, and a magazine columnist. He presented the six-part BBC-TV series *Last Chance to See*, with actor Stephen Fry, in which the unlikely duo travelled the world in search of a motley collection of endangered species (following in the footsteps of a similar journey Mark made with author Douglas Adams 20 years earlier). For many years, Mark presented the weekly half-hour programme *Nature* on BBC Radio 4, and he has written more than 50 books on a variety of wildlife and conservation subjects.

Foreword

What's the best wildlife encounter in the world? Well, it all depends... My luckiest encounter was undoubtedly in Wolong, southwestern China, when a giant panda unexpectedly stepped out of the bamboo forest right in front of me. We stared at one another for a full two seconds – two whole earth-shattering, hair-raising, life-changing seconds with a real-life wild giant panda – before it ambled back into oblivion never to be seen again (not by me, and probably not by anyone else on the planet).

But how can you compare that with the adrenalin rush of a face-to-face underwater encounter with a hungry tiger shark in the Bahamas? Or the sheer delight in tickling a 30-tonne grey whale under the chin in Mexico (I've done that more often than I can remember, but it still reduces me to a gibbering wreck every time)? How about breathlessly stalking a southern white rhino on foot, or the sheer spectacle of South Georgia's avian Glastonbury, with 150,000 pairs of king penguins on a single beach?

Bigger isn't necessarily better. I remember once in Arizona putting on red lipstick (it was the first and only time I have ever worn make-up of any kind), puckering up my lips, and crossing my fingers in the hope that nobody would see me. Oh, and my mouth was full of sickly-sweet sugar-water. I was hummingbird-watching and, in a heartbeat, there were blurred shapes like bees on speed, whizzing backwards and forwards in front of my face. One particular hummingbird – a Costa's, with iridescent purple flares like a flashy moustache – hovered right in front of my face with the immaculate precision of a helicopter pilot. Very carefully, it put its beak right inside my mouth, and drank. I could feel its wingbeats against my cheeks. Wildlife encounters don't come much closer, or more thrilling, than that.

The truth is that all wildlife encounters are 'the best'. After more than 30 years spent criss-crossing the globe, and countless millions of air miles, I haven't lost one scintilla of the original passion and wonderment that first plunged me into the world of wildlife. I know I am not alone when I say that I need to see wildlife just to survive normal daily life. It doesn't have to be exotic or far away. I never think 'oh, it's just a robin', or 'it's just a rabbit'. The other day, I was watching a badger emerge from its urban sett – right next to the platform at my local railway station. It popped its head out and peered at all the commuters a few metres away, before having a scratch and running off into someone's garden. It made my whole day.

Quite simply, wildlife of any kind is good for the soul.

Wildlife watching can be good for the wildlife, too. I firmly believe that responsible ecotourism can be an invaluable conservation tool. It makes wildlife worth more alive than dead, by raising much-needed foreign exchange for cash-strapped governments, providing employment for local people (everything from anti-poaching patrols in Kenya to carving wooden Komodo dragons to sell to tourists in Indonesia) and, managed properly, raises funds for the upkeep of national parks and reserves. But it's more than that. Everything doesn't have to be measured in financial terms alone. Responsible ecotourism also helps to rekindle a concern for wildlife and a sense of wonderment that many people seem to have lost. The closer people feel to wildlife, the more they care about its well-being.

Let's face it. The world's wildlife needs all the help it can get. We have already lost countless species, and many more are teetering on the brink. The point is that we cannot rely on an aye-aye to worry about the wellbeing of a snow leopard, or a mountain gorilla to look out for a whale shark. Only we can do that. And through a combination of indifference, incompetence, ignorance and greed, we are failing to do it properly. We need more people who care.

Amy has done a wonderful job in compiling this wide-ranging collection of, by any measure, some of the best wildlife encounters in the world. The result is a fantastic potpourri of hundreds of weird and wonderful animals – from aardvarks and fossa to magnificent frigatebirds and blue whales – with top tips on where and when to spot them in the wild.

I hope, if you're lucky enough to have seen some of them already, the book will bring back many happy memories. If you haven't, I'm sure it will inspire you to go and look for them. But these are also encounters to dream about. Nothing beats searching for whales with the wind in your hair, tracking wild dogs with African dust clinging to your boots, or cruising past a polar bear with your fingers numb with the cold. But, sometimes, it is enough just knowing that all those otters, platypuses, manatees, giant tortoises, brown bears and all the other awe-inspiring, captivating, remarkable animals in this book are out there, wild and free.

by **Mark Carwardine**

Contents

Aardvark *Orycteropus afer*

WHAT The name translates as 'earth-pig', but while true pigs are hoofed mammals, this secretive ant guzzler is in a group of its own. A night safari is essential if your heart is set on an encounter. You might meet one on its nightly rounds, where it uses senses of hearing and smell so acute that vision is almost redundant. That comical snout contains arguably the most complex olfactory apparatus in the animal kingdom, and the area of an aardvark's brain dedicated to smelling is hugely enlarged. Having sniffed out an ant or termite mound, the aardvark uses sharp, hooflike claws to break in, then slurps up prey with its long, sticky tongue. **WHERE** Several reserves in the South African Karoo offer specialist aardvark tours, aiming to track their resident aardvarks as they snuffle between ant or termite mounds.

© Jonathan Gregson | Lonely Planet, © Michael Heffernan | Lonely Planet

African savannah elephant *Loxodonta africana*

WHAT If the lion is Africa's king of beasts, this magnificent pachyderm, the world's largest land animal, might be its high priestess. Elephant society is orderly, cooperative, empathetic and matriarchal, and an encounter in the wild leaves you in no doubt you've been touched by greatness – three to six tonnes of it. Elephants make an equally big impression on the landscapes they occupy. Their feeding habits play a major part in maintaining the characteristic open woodland of the savannah, and stimulating regrowth of the trees they push down or rip up. **WHERE** The once vast range of the plains elephants across eastern and southern Africa is increasingly fragmented by human development, but responsible elephant tourism has an important role to play in improving a strained relationship between the species and human communities. The largest remaining population is in Botswana's Chobe National Park.

THE A-Z OF WILDLIFE WATCHING

African wild dog
Lycaon pictus

WHAT Loping through the savannah, a pack of African wild dogs is one of the most accomplished hunting teams in the natural world. The lithe canines, standing up to 75cm tall at the shoulder, run their prey – often gazelles – to ground over long distances, with an 80% success rate. Despite their prowess, they're increasingly endangered and just 5000 survive in the wild, mostly in southern Africa and the south of east Africa. **WHERE** Selous Game Reserve, Tanzania is vast (50,000 sq km) but in July and August African wild dogs will be staying close to their dens to care for pups and will be easier for a guide to track. The rest of the year the nomadic packs will be running down impala in the park. Niassa Reserve in Mozambique also supports a significant population of the dogs and May to July is the optimum time to visit.

Alligator (American) *Alligator mississippiensis*

WHAT Perhaps the closest thing to a prehistoric encounter is to visit one of the many wildlife parks and refuges where American alligators now thrive. Having suffered severe declines due to hunting and habitat loss in the early and mid-20th century, the species has responded well to protection and is no longer endangered. **WHERE** The natural range of the American alligator takes in a swathe of wetland across the southeastern US, from Texas to the Florida Everglades, where it plays an important role in wetland ecology, creating small ponds ('gator holes') that retain water even in dry periods. In places like Big Cypress National Preserve at Ochopee, Florida, you're almost guaranteed to find one resting on or close to a walkway. It's a tempting photo opportunity, but there's no room for complacency – those jaws mean business.

Alpine chough *Pyrrhocorax graculus*

WHAT There's something enviable about the life of an alpine chough. Not only do these exuberant crows have a rich social life and a lifelong pair bond, they live in some of the world's most spectacular locations, exploiting mountain air currents with spectacularly acrobatic flight. Even their yellow beaks and red legs appear to be a reminder not to take life too seriously. The fun belies the fact that these are seriously hardy birds – capable of nesting at up to 6500m and cruising the upper slopes of Mt Everest at over 8200m. **WHERE** You can make your chough quest as challenging as you like. There are relatively accessible flocks in places like Hecho Valley in the Pyrenees, others in the Alps, Balkans, Atlas and Caucasus mountains, but you can also see them in the high Himalayas, where they are often spotted at Everest base camp.

Alpine ibex *Capra ibex*

WHAT One of nine closely related species of wild goat, the Alpine ibex has earned special affection as an early conservation success and for its jaw-dropping displays of nerve and agility. **WHERE** Like all wild goats, Alpine ibex are at home on steep ground and spend much of the year grazing above the treeline on rocky terrain where their dull brown coats provide excellent camouflage. Nowhere is this agility demonstrated to more breathtaking effect than at Cingino Dam in Italy's Gran Paradiso National Park, where goats scale the near-vertical dam wall to access mineral salts leaching from the rock. Gran Paradiso and the connected Vanoise National Park in France were established specifically to protect the Alpine ibex, and the expanding populations now seen across much of the Alpine region are descended from those that survived here in the early 20th century.

THE A-Z OF WILDLIFE WATCHING

American bison *Bison bison*

WHAT Declared America's first national mammal by President Obama in 2016, the American bison (or buffalo, for romantics and Wild West fans) carries the weight of celebrity lightly on its massive shoulders. A large male weighs up to a metric tonne, but sustains its massive bulk on nothing more than grasses and sedges. In many ways, bison are the prairies – their heavy grazing and occasional scuffing is essential in maintaining the diversity of ground flora that characterises this unique ecosystem. **WHERE** North America's largest mammal once dominated prairie habitats from the Canadian northwest to Mexico. Only fragments of those vast herds can now be seen, but they are expanding thanks to conservation and ecotourism. The largest herd to be seen today numbers about 5000 animals and is to be found in Yellowstone National Park, where a visit can help safeguard their future.

Anaconda
Eunectes murinus

WHAT A colossus among reptiles, the green anaconda is the world's heaviest and second-longest snake, though wild specimens are almost impossible to measure with accuracy. Suffice to say, a large individual can exceed 5m, grow as thick as a child's torso and weigh 100kg or more – depending when, and what, it last ate. Most prey (fish, birds, caiman and mammals as large as deer, tapir and capybara) are caught by aquatic stealth and subdued by constriction, and everything is swallowed whole. **WHERE** Despite its size, in swamps, pools and sluggish streams of the Amazon and Orinoco Basin, you could pass within touching distance of a green anaconda slipping smoothly and silently through weedy water and not know it. The specimens in Ecuador's Yasuni National Park are among the largest and best-studied, thanks to the respect the species is given by the local Waorani people.

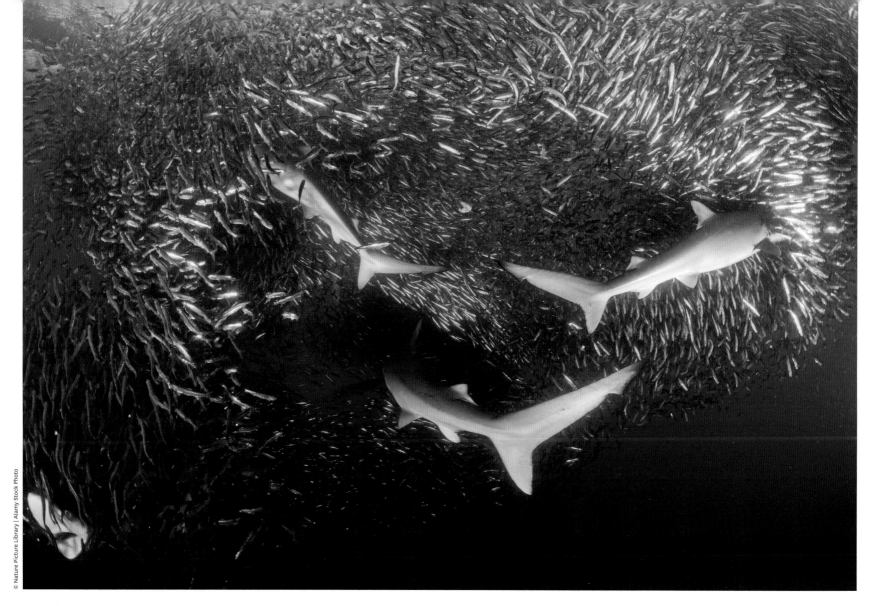

Anchovy (school) *Engraulis spp*

WHAT This quicksilver maelstrom of life may be the greatest spectacle of numbers in the oceans. Anchovies are one of the world's most numerous fish, and they're on everyone's menu. Migrating shoals up to 10 million strong are targeted by predators including Chinook salmon, sailfish, sharks, sea lions, humpback whales, penguins, gannets and pelicans, all with their own jaw-dropping hunting techniques; feeding doesn't get any more frenzied. Of the nine *Engraulis* genus of anchovy, the European, Californian, Southern African, Japanese, Argentine and Peruvian are also targeted by humans; the latter is caught in greater numbers than any other fish. **WHERE** Large anchovy shoals gather in nutrient-rich upwellings along the southeastern Pacific, sometimes tracked by the ocean research stations at Monterey Bay and La Jolla in California. Anchovy schools are also part of many South African shark tours.

Andean Condor *Vultur gryphus*

WHAT A jumbo jet of a bird, the Andean condor is the largest living animal capable of self-propelled flight. Wingtip to wingtip it measures up to 3.3m, and weighs anything up to 15kg. This kind of bulk takes a lot of lifting and thus the species favours habitats with reliable winds or strong thermal updrafts, such as mountains, coasts and deserts. Condors are the New World equivalent of vultures, and feed mainly on carrion, including dead cattle and other livestock. The bald head is a hygienic adaptation to unavoidably messy mealtimes.

WHERE There are condor hotspots along much of the Andean chain, with lofty viewing points offering the opportunity to appreciate the full grandeur of both the birds and their habitat. Try Peru's Colca Canyon, the Argentine Lake District or Torres del Paine National Park in Chile.

Antechinus
Antechinus spp

WHAT Spare a thought for the male antechinus. For 50 weeks of the year this grey, mouse-like marsupial feeds continuously on bugs, moving so quickly around the trees of its temperate rainforest habitat in Australia that it appears to teleport. Then, in July or August – the depths of the Australian winter – a switch is flicked and every male antechinus becomes intensely focused on one thing only: finding and mating with as many females as possible. They don't eat or rest and two weeks later, their bodies overwhelmed by stress hormones, every male is dead. The females live long enough to raise the next hyperactive generation. There are up to 15 species of antechinus, with three species only recently discovered, distributed from Queensland's tropics to the Tasman peninsula. **WHERE** Springbrook National Park in Queensland is easily accessible from Brisbane and the Gold Coast and home to several species. They are less inhibited during mating season.

Arabian oryx *Oryx leucoryx*

WHAT Said to be the origin of unicorn myths (side views sometimes only show one horn), the Arabian oryx was headed for the same state of non-existence in the late 20th century. But thanks to a captive breeding and reintroduction effort beginning in the 1960s, this svelte white antelope became the first species to have its conservation status downgraded from extinct in the wild to vulnerable. The global population now numbers several thousand, but free-living herds still struggle due to poaching, overgrazing and geochemical exploitation of their arid habitats. **WHERE** The best chances of seeing oryx in natural habitat is to visit a reintroduction reserve such as Wadi Rum or Shaumari in Jordan, Sir Bani Yas Island in Abu Dhabi, the Dubai Desert Conservation Reserve, or the area around Ein Shahak, Israel. These populations vary in the extent of their freedom, with most fenced or tagged for protection and research.

Arctic tern *Sterna paradisaea*

WHAT Consider yourself a big traveller? Dainty-looking Arctic terns make an annual round trip of up to 90,000km from northern breeding grounds to southern feeding areas – by far the longest migration of any animal. Juveniles may make the journey south at less than three months of age. They are distinguished from the similar-looking common tern by their all-red bill – that of the common tern has a black tip. Identification is trickier from a distance though, leading some birders to use the shared nickname 'comic tern'. **WHERE** Arctic terns breed around northern coasts of Europe, Asia and North America, and it's here that you have the best chances to see them. For a truly intimate encounter, visit the Farne Islands off northeast England in early summer, but wear a hat – anxious parent birds will dive-bomb any perceived threat.

Argali
Ovis ammon

WHAT Crash! That's the sound of two male argali battling in mating season. The argali of Central Asia has evolved to be the largest wild sheep; males have colossal corkscrew horns weighing up to 20kg, gaining a ring for every year of age. During the mating season the mountain slopes and steppes ring to the sound of clashing males. One of the several sub-species of argali is named the Marco Polo sheep, named after the explorer who described them in 1273, when they roamed central Asia in huge numbers. Hunting and poaching has since caused the argali to become critically endangered. In some conservancies, traditional hunters now protect the sheep from poaching. **WHERE** The Tajikistan Mountain Ungulate Project, a merging of six community-based conservancies, is home to about 500 Marco Polo sheep. One such conservancy is Burgut in the mountainous Alichur region bordering Afghanistan, Pakistan and China. Use local homestays and hire Burgut rangers as guides.

Armadillo
Dasypus novemcinctus

WHAT Aztecs knew this eccentric-looking creature as *āyōtōchtli*, literally meaning 'turtle rabbit'. Armadillos are the only mammals with a bony carapace, a strange armour growing within the skin of the back and flanks and covered with horny scales. The carapace is articulated by the bands for which several species are named (count them), and which allow the animal to roll up defensively. The nine-banded armadillo forages mainly around dusk and dawn, but may emerge in full daylight on cooler days. They are docile, but think twice before handling them – these are the only non-human mammals known to carry leprosy. **WHERE** The nine-banded armadillo is widespread from the Brazilian Pantanal to Texas, where it is the official state small mammal and can be spotted in reserve areas such as Palmetto Park in Gonzales and the Lost Maples State Natural Area near Vanderpool.

© Leah Smalley | Shutterstock

Asiatic elephant
Elephas maximus

WHAT Three subspecies of Asian elephant are recognised – the Indian, Sri-Lankan and Sumatran. While an encounter with these magnificent animals might easily be the highlight of a trip, there is an ugly side to elephant tourism in Asia. More than 30% of the world's Asian elephants live in captivity, often having 'retired' from the logging industry, and welfare conditions vary greatly. Avoid operators offering rides or any kind of show in which elephants are required to perform. The population on Bali are all introduced for tourism purposes. For a truly rewarding and ethical elephant encounter, you may need to accept the more hit-and-miss nature of watching them in the wild.

WHERE Wild elephants can be seen with reputable guides in Chitwan and Bardia National Parks in Nepal, Corbett National Park in India and Khao Yai National Park in Thaliand.

Atlantic goliath grouper
Epinephalus itajara

WHAT A hulking mottled form hoves slowly into view, its dinner plate-sized fins fanning the water. At more than 2m long and weighing 300kg, this king among grouper seems cumbersome – until it strikes. The sudden opening of a cavernous mouth easily engulfs prey half as long as the grouper itself – crabs, lobsters, bony fish and small sharks. Diving with grouper can be a multisensory experience – startled individuals are able to release a booming alarm by vibrating the air-filled swimbladder.

WHERE Its range includes the Bahamas, the Caribbean and the Brazilian coast, but south Florida has seen a rise in goliath grouper numbers in recent decades, thanks to tighter regulation of fishing. Huge individuals patrol many popular reef and wreck dive sites, and in August and September spawning aggregations off Jupiter and West Palm Beach attract not only groupers, but huge schools of smaller fish, which feed on the clouds of eggs.

© imageBROKER / Alamy Stock Photo

© Christian Schweiger | 500px

Atlantic puffin *Fratercula arctica*

WHAT With an appearance somewhere between cartoonish and handsome, Atlantic puffins in breeding colours are among the most popular seabird visitors to coasts of Newfoundland, Greenland, Iceland, Scandinavia and Britain. They breed in clifftop burrows or other crevices, favouring islands without ground predators. As summer wanes they return to the open sea, discarding their garish beak plates and eye ornaments and becoming unrecognisably drab. **WHERE** Productive seas and the complex rocky northern and western coastlines of the British Isles are ideal for puffins, but large colonies are restricted to islands where adults and young are safe from terrestrial predators. There are good populations on Skomer in west Wales and at Hermaness, Sumburgh and Noss in the Shetland Isles. On the mainland coasts they favour cliff ledges over clifftop burrows, such as those at Bempton in North Yorkshire.

THE A-Z OF WILDLIFE WATCHING

Atlas moth *Attacus atlas*

WHAT With a wingspan exceeding 25cm, this velvety goliath of an insect is one of the world's largest moths (only outdone in size by the Hercules). Its glory is short-lived however, as the adults are unable to feed and rarely survive more than two weeks, a brief interlude in which their only priority is reproduction. Females rest close to the chrysalis from which they emerge, wafting pheromones into the night air and waiting for males to find them. Despite their huge wings, atlas moths are poor fliers, and their best defence is a bluff; the pattern of the wingtips resembles the head of a cobra. **WHERE** Atlas moths are relatively common in dry tropical forests of Southeast Asia, especially Malaysia. Citrus and cinnamon groves are a good bet, and an exploration of the mangroves of the Sungei Buloh Wetland Reserve in Singapore often yields resting moths and their great pale shaggy caterpillars by day, and blundering, lovelorn males after dark.

Axolotl *Ambystoma mexicanum*

WHAT The spectacular diversity of modern terrestrial vertebrates owes much to the ancient amphibian ancestor that made the momentous transition from water to dry land. But for this Mexican salamander, the move was overrated, and it has dispensed with the metamorphosis from aquatic larva to land-dwelling, air-breathing adult and opted for life as a fully aquatic Peter Pan, maturing in larval form. The isolation that allowed this regressive evolution to take place now also threatens the species' survival, as human development engulfs the two high-altitude lakes in which it was known. **WHERE** Drastic recent declines in wild axolotl numbers in the species' last known location in Lake Xochimilco in Mexico City have prompted emergency conservation measures. Sadly, so little remains of the original lake habitat that the future for the species is uncertain.

THE A-Z OF WILDLIFE WATCHING

Aye-aye
Daubentonia madagascariensis

WHAT Madagascar is a hothouse of evolution, where ecological niches are not always occupied by the usual suspects. These wonderfully weird lemurs perform the role of woodpeckers in the island's remaining rainforests and also visit cultivated land – where their disconcerting presence is not always welcome. Their grizzled shaggy fur, hypnotic eyes, bat ears and the creepiest middle finger in the animal kingdom make them something of a night-terror in Malagasy folk tradition. In fact the spindly digit, which rotates on a ball-and socket joint, is a specialised tool, used for sounding out tree cavities containing wood-boring grubs. Once prey is detected, a hole is opened with rodent-like teeth and the bugs winkled out with the longer fourth finger.

WHERE The tiny island reserve of Akanin'ny nofy is home to several aye-ayes unusually habituated to humans, and there is a good population at the Farankaraina Forestry Reserve near Maroantsetra.

© Justin Foulkes | Lonely Planet

Babirusa
Babyrousa spp

WHAT Babirusas are pigs, but pigs unlike any other. What was considered a single species was recently split into three, living on different Indonesian islands. A proposed fourth species, described from long-dead remains, may still be living in parts of Sulawesi – a mystery begging for further zoological exploration. The distinctive curving upper canines of the best known and most widespread species grow throughout life, piercing the lip and curving back towards the forehead. In very long-lived males, it is possible for these tusks to ultimately pierce the unfortunate animal's own skull.

WHERE Babirusa are endemic to the Indonesian archipelagos and islands of Sulawesi, Togian, Sula and Buru. Pleistocene cave paintings near Maros on Sulawesi suggest the species was significant to early modern humans living in the area 35,000 years ago. To see them live in the region today your best bet to is head to Nantu National Nature Preserve on Sulawesi.

Bactrian camel *Camelus ferus*

WHAT One hump or two? This is the only camel remaining in a truly wild state and is now considered a separate species not only from the one-humped dromedary, but also from the domesticated Bactrian. And if other camels have a reputation for toughness, they haven't met the wild Bactrian – the only mammal able to drink salt water and survive a staggering temperature range of -28 to 38°C. Despite this impressive toughness the species is still sadly classified as *Critically Endangered*, with roughly 1000 individuals living in the wild.

WHERE Wild Bactrian camels are now restricted to the border region between Mongolia and China's Xinjiang province. Both nations have established reserves in which the camels are strictly protected and a captive breeding and reintroduction programme is underway at the Zakhyn Us Sanctuary in Mongolia's Great Gobi Reserve.

Bald eagle *Haliaeetus leucocephalus*

WHAT Even novice birdwatchers should have no trouble identifying this North American icon, also one of the 20th century's great conservation success stories. Breeding sites are invariably within striking distance of open water – and the colossal nests required to support families are sited in tall trees within mature forest. Bald eagles are early breeders and their spectacular courtship, involving calls and tumbling tandem display flights, often take place in late winter whilst snow still lies on the ground. **WHERE** Bald eagle sightings are now possible almost anywhere on the North American continent, from Alaska and much of northern Canada to Mexico. The largest breeding populations are in Alaska and British Columbia, but well over 1000 pairs breed in both Minnesota and Florida, and in 2015 a pair made the first breeding attempt in New York City for 100 years, on Staten Island.

Barn owl
Tyto alba

WHAT Despite its gigantic global range (among the largest of any bird), the barn owl retains an aura of mystique, due in part to its ghostly colouration, monkish face and lighter-than-air flight, which is rendered completely silent by the fine-fringed margins of the principal flight feathers. In Europe and North America, agricultural buildings are the species' favoured breeding sites, and they are welcome on farmland because of their prodigious appetite for rats and mice – their high metabolic rate means that weight for weight they consume more prey than any other predator of rodents. **WHERE** The barn owl is one of few species you can see wild and native on six continents. Aim for tussocky or unimproved grassland habitats including pasture and steppe, during the hours of dawn and dusk.

© Alfredo Maiquez | Shutterstock

© Jill Cooper | Alamy Stock Photo

© All Canada Photos | Alamy Stock Photo

Beaver *Castor spp (C canadensis and C fiber)*

WHAT The word rodent comes from the Latin rodere, meaning 'to gnaw'. It's an ability exemplified by the two species of beaver, whose orange, chisel-like incisors make short work of felling anything from saplings to mature trees. Felled timber is stored underwater as a winter food resource or used to construct lodges and dams, resulting in some drastic habitat engineering. While watching beavers, take the opportunity to appreciate the biodiverse mosaic of wetland, meadow, and woodland they create. The impact is most obvious in those parts of Europe to which beaver species have been restored in recent years. **WHERE** Beaver numbers are increasing on both sides of the Atlantic thanks to active conservation. Popular beaver tours operate at the Malingsbo-Kloten Nature Reserve in Sweden, and the Eurasian beaver has been successfully reintroduced to more than 25 other countries, most of which have viewing opportunities.

THE A-Z OF WILDLIFE WATCHING

Beluga whale *Delphinapterus leucas*

WHAT Watching belugas or white whales is a two-way process. These highly social, cooperative and playful cetaceans often appear as fascinated by humans as we are by them. Their flexible lips allow them to pull a variety of facial expressions, including smiles, and they are exceptionally vocal, with a range of calls including clicks, whistles and bird-like chirps, earning them their nickname 'sea canary'. **WHERE** The white whale has a circum-polar distribution in shallow seas and estuaries on coasts of Eurasia and North America. Individuals and groups occasionally travel far up rivers and live for months at a time in entirely fresh water. The population around Churchill on Canada's Hudson Bay is particularly accessible, with opportunities to watch from boats, or to kayak and even snorkel among the whales.

Bighorn sheep *Ovis canadensis*

WHAT It's called head-butting, but battles between rival bighorn rams are a whole-body effort. Contenders are muscular and agile, and throw themselves at one another with such spectacular force that the impact of bone on bone is often audible more than a mile away. Battles may last anything from seconds to 24 hours. Outside the mating season, small herds can become very inconspicuous, grazing placidly on precipitous slopes where they often blend perfectly with surrounding landscapes. **WHERE** Bighorns are native to western North America, with distinct subspecies occupying the deserts of the southwestern US and Mexico (Mojave, Sornoran and Colorado), the Sierra Nevada and the Rockies. They can be viewed on tours run by the National Bighorn Sheep Interpretive Center at Dubois, Wyoming.

Bilby
Macrotis lagrotis

WHAT With comically large ears, two powerful hind legs, greyish fur and a preference for living in burrows, the bilby is Australia's indigenous stand-in for the Easter Bunny. But there the similarities with rabbits end. The omnivorous Greater bilby is the largest member of the bandicoot family. It's a marsupial, with a rear-facing pouch that typically accommodates about three young at a time. Adult males weigh up to 2.5kg and are 50cm in length, females are about half that size. They feed on seeds, insects, fruit, fungi and small creatures in their natural habitat of desert shrub and grasslands of Western Australia and the Northern Territory.

WHERE Being nocturnal and highly endangered, seeing a bilby in the wild is unlikely. Currawinya National Park in southwest Queensland is home to a growing community of protected bilbies but their enclosure is off-limits to visitors. Instead, visit The Bilby Centre in Charleville, Queensland.

© Minden Pictures | Alamy Stock Photo

© Nobuo Matsumura | Alamy Stock Photo

© Matt Munro | Lonely Planet

Birds of paradise *Paradisaeidae spp*

WHAT When naturalist Sir David Attenborough does your public relations, your show better not disappoint. Fortunately, with forty species of birds of paradise endemic to the island of New Guinea, there's no chance of that. Footage of these birds' choreographed mating dances and eye-popping plumage was first shown on Attenborough's *Life on Earth* TV series. Of the species, some of the most spectacular are the King of Saxony, with its two long blue quills sprouting from its forehead (found in the Central Ranges of New Guinea), the Raggiana bird of paradise (above), with its gauzy display (see the lowlands of southern New Guinea), and the Superb bird of paradise, with its iridescent collar (found in the mid-mountains of the Central Ranges and the Huon Peninsula). **WHERE** Several outfitters run bird-watching tours to Papua New Guinea but the costs can be high. Independent travellers are able to use a birding guidebook but take local advice.

THE A-Z OF WILDLIFE WATCHING

Birdwing butterfly (Queen Alexandra's) *Ornithoptera alexandrae*

WHAT With a wingspan of more than 25cm, the world's largest butterfly is said to resemble a bird in flight. The largest individuals are the black and cream females. The males, while smaller, are arguably more breathtaking still, with dazzling turquoise, black and gold wings. **WHERE T**he Managalas Plateau in Oro Province, northern Papua New Guinea is an ambitious destination – and even now, western travellers are extremely few. But the plateau is one of few places where this sensational species (known as *dadakul* in the local Jimun language) can be seen in the wild. In a region threatened by development for palm oil plantations and where traditional livelihoods are marginal, some see butterfly ecotourism as a potential solution. Plans to protect the area for conservation are being considered by the national government.

Bittern
Botaurus stellaris

WHAT Some species you sense with the eyes, others delight the ear. This cryptic heron covers both, but the first place most people sense a bittern is in their gut. The call of a male is so deep it resembles the boom of an underground explosion, or the bass throb of a distant nightclub. The challenge then becomes visual. Bittern plumage offers exceptional camouflage amongst their preferred reedbed habitat, and the disappearing act is enhanced by wary birds adopting what looks like a yoga posture, beak pointing skyward to align with the vertical stems around it. The pose is known as 'bitterning'.

WHERE Bitterns are challenging to spot, but opportunities are increasing as wetland restoration projects take place. Try the huge rewilded Oostvaardersplassen in the Netherlands, the London Wetland Centre in the UK or Rocca al Mare Beach in Tallinn, Estonia.

Black heron
Egretta ardesiaca

WHAT Dressed in funereal black, this small heron hunts with the exaggerated cloak-and-dagger dastardliness of a pantomime villain. Known as 'canopy feeding' the routine would be comical were it not so deadly effective. A stalking bird uses its wings to shade the water, creating an illusion of shelter, below which its yellow feet twitch just enough to attract the attention of small fish and amphibians. Alas for those tempted close, the shading also reduces reflections from the water surface and makes it easy for the heron to spear itself a meal. **WHERE** Black herons can be seen in much of Eastern and Southern Africa and Madagascar. Shallow-edged lakes such as Siwandu in the Selous Game Reserve in Tanzania are best for observing their feeding behaviour; for coastal roosts try the Marine National Parks of Kenya's Malindi-Watamu Biosphere Reserve.

Black panther *Panthera pardus*

WHAT A black panther is a genetic variant of either a leopard (or, less commonly, a jaguar) in which the coat is all dark due to over-production of the pigment melanin. Often the coat is dark brown rather than black, and in good light you'll see that they still have the rosettes of black spots that characterise gold-coated leopards; these show up very clearly through an infra-red viewer. **WHERE** Melanistic leopards are relatively common in heavily forested parts of the species' range such as Indonesia (especially Java), the Malay Peninsula, Myanmar, Nepal and the northeastern and southern states of Assam and Kerala in India. African examples are much less common, except on the forested slopes of Mt Kenya.

Black rhinoceros
Diceros bicornis

WHAT The generally solitary black rhino feeds mainly on shoots and leaves plucked with its distinctive hooked upper lip. Lip-shape is the best way to tell the species apart from its square-lipped cousin, the so-called white rhino, since both are actually indistinguishably grey. The conservation status of the species is desperate, with 97.6% of the population disappearing from 1960 to the '90s, but 11th-hour conservation is proving effective in some heavily protected areas. The species' reputation for aggression is only partly deserved, and many reserves are confident enough to offer low-impact walking safaris – arguably the most thrilling way to encounter these magnificent mammals. **WHERE** Ol Pejeta Conservancy in Laikipia, northern Kenya, is the largest rhino sanctuary in the world, with more than 100 resident black rhinos. The less-visited game reserves of Selous in Tanzania and Madikwe in South Africa are rapidly gaining reputations as places to see the species.

© JT Platt | Shutterstock

Black footed ferret
Mustela nigripes

WHAT The only ferret native to the Americas was declared extinct in 1979 – prematurely, as it turned out. Two years later a small population was discovered at Meeteetse, Wyoming, but this dwindled alarmingly and the last 18 individuals were taken into captivity, where their descendants have been bred ever since to stock an ongoing reintroduction programme. Today there are around 370 of these handsome mustelids at 28 locations in the wild, in the US, Canada and Mexico. Every site has good populations of prairie dogs, on which the ferrets depend for prey and for burrows.

WHERE The survival of the species is far from assured and opportunities to see them in the wild are limited for conservation reasons. However they can be spotted in Aubrey Valley, near Seligman in Arizona, and with luck in Wind Cave and Badlands National Parks in South Dakota, and in the American Prairie Reserve in Montana.

Black tipped reef shark *Carcharhinus melanopterus*

WHAT If you've been diving or snorkelling in the tropical waters of the Indo-Pacific oceans, there's a good chance you've been around blacktip reef sharks. These relatively numerous requiem sharks can congregate in large numbers in shallow waters around coral reefs, hunting such fish as mullet and even octopus and crustaceans. They're small, at around 1.5m in length, but what they lack in stature they make up for with numbers and they'll sometimes cooperate to corral shoals of reef fish before feeding. They give birth to live pups, which spend their first year in nurseries. **WHERE** It's often possible to see these sharks when snorkelling or diving in places in such places as the Maldives, Micronesia and Bora Bora. Beqa Lagoon in Fiji offers almost guaranteed sightings, although their larger relatives, tiger and bull sharks, also lurk here.

Blue morpho butterfly *Morpho peleides*

WHAT With electric blue wings spanning 12-20cm, the blue morpho is among the world's most conspicuous and exciting butterflies. Its dazzling colour is produced not by pigment, but by the complex nanostructure of the wing scales, which selectively reflects and reinforces blue wavelengths of light. Only the upper wings produce this iridescence – the underwings are camouflaged in mottled brown, so that insects in flight seem to flicker magically in and out of existence. **WHERE** Morphos occur in forest habitats throughout Latin America, and the rainforest reserves of Costa Rica are a great place to look. Numbers vary seasonally, with a rainy season peak on the Pacific side (for example Corcovado National Park) while dry season numbers are higher on the Caribbean side – try the peninsular National Park of Cahuita.

THE A-Z OF WILDLIFE WATCHING

Blue whale *Balaenoptera musculus*

WHAT Twenty years ago a tour operator touting opportunities to glimpse, let alone swim with, the largest animal that has ever lived on Earth would have been regarded with derision. But following the global moratorium on hunting, numbers of these stupendous cetaceans are up, sightings are way up, and with the aid of technology such as GPS tags and camera drones, we know more about their lives and movements than 20th-century zoologists might have dreamed. **WHERE** Blue whales are truly cosmopolitan mammals, recorded in all the world's oceans and virtually all adjoining seas. Distinct populations feed in polar seas in summer and travel to warmer waters to calve in winter. Hotspots for blue whale-watching include the Azores, the St Lawrence River in Quebec, Monterey Bay in California, Baja California in Mexico and around Sri Lanka.

Blue-footed booby
Sula nebouxii

WHAT Male blue-footed boobies are inordinately proud of their feet, and with good reason – the colour is used by females to judge the quality of potential mates. Biologically speaking this makes sense, as the blue hue derives from carotenoid pigments acquired from prey. The same pigments also function in immunity, so an azure-footed suitor is probably well fed, healthy and likely to provide well for a family. If a male doesn't eat well, his feet begin to fade within days, and his weakness shows. Harsh, but honest.

WHERE Blue-foots can be seen on Pacific coasts and islands from California to Peru. The tiny Galapagos island of North Seymour is home to a large breeding colony between June and August, and close views of nesting birds can be had from the short visitor trail.

Bonobo
Pan paniscus

WHAT With 98.8% genetic similarity to humans, bonobos and chimpanzees are our closest living relatives. This kinship is most apparent in the personal interactions of the highly social, cooperative, communicative and empathetic bonobo. Many of their facial expressions and gestures appear to translate across the species barrier and there's no doubt about it, eye contact is a meeting of minds. **WHERE** Bonobos live only in the Democratic Republic of Congo, south of the Congo River. Visiting the area is a major expedition, and while safari opportunities are opening up after years of war in the region, encounters with wild bonobos remain the preserve of primatologists. However, it is possible to visit the world's only bonobo sanctuary, Lola ya Bonobo, near Kinshasa, where injured or orphaned bonobos are rehabilitated for release back to the wild. And reports suggest that Iyondji Community Bonobo Reserve in the DRC will soon allow wildlife tourism.

Bottlenose dolphin *Tursiops truncatus* and *T aduncus*

WHAT This best known and loved of small cetaceans has become a celebrity in both popular culture and scientific circles, exhibiting intelligence and behaviour that continue to surprise. They are social, self-aware, highly communicative, playful and capable of tool use, teamwork, mimicry and intense curiosity. Combined with extraordinary athleticism, these traits make them a joy to watch – and a highly achievable must-see on any bucket list. **WHERE** Bottlenose dolphins are found in warm and temperate seas around the world. What was until recently regarded as one species was split in the 1990s into the common bottlenose found in Atlantic and offshore waters, and the Indo-Pacific species, generally associated with coasts and estuaries. Hybrids almost certainly occur in areas where the two species meet, among them the Burrunan dolphin found in parts of Victoria, Australia and recognised as a species in 2011.

© Konrad Wothe | Getty Images

Brown bear *Ursus arctos*

WHAT For 'brown' read almost any shade of cream, buff, blond, red, mustard, tawny, grey, chocolate or near black. Brown bears also vary greatly in size, weighing anything from 130-600kg as adults. But even the smallest demand respect. Bright clothing and bells on backpacks or clothing are a sensible precaution when moving about, and keep pepper spray to hand. **WHERE** Brown bears have by far the largest range of any bear species, with more than a dozen distinct subspecies across much of the northern hemisphere. Bear enthusiasts are especially well catered for at the Kodiak National Wildlife Refuge in Alaska and at the Wild Brown Bear Centre near Vartius on the Finland-Russian border, where safe hides and the midnight summer sun allow bear-watching around the clock.

Brown kiwi
Apteryx australis

WHAT A rotund, brown shape is ambling along the shoreline of the beach, stopping frequently to probe for food with its long beak. Of the five species of kiwi – which has lent its name to New Zealanders in general – one of the largest sub-species is the tokoeka of Stewart Island, which is also known as Rakiura. This kiwi is also notable for being the only variety to forage in daylight, making it slightly easier to spot than its shy South Island cousins and Northern Brown relative. The Stewart Island kiwi numbers 10,000 or more due to its relative protection on the island; other ground-dwelling birds in New Zealand are not so fortunate.

WHERE New Zealand's third largest island, off the tip of South Island, can be reached by ferry or plane, with both crossings liable to be turbulent. There are several wildlife and kiwi-spotting tours available on the island but also strict rules about approaching wild animals.

Budgerigar *Melopsittacus undulatus*

WHAT In a wild flock, all the characteristics for which captive budgerigars are known and loved are amplified. Their social nature is fully expressed in flocks numbering a few dozen to several thousand, their talkativeness and mimicry is used extensively to communicate and impress, and their vibrant colouration becomes a mass spectacle. To our eyes, they appear tri-coloured, with a yellow head, green body and blue tail, but the birds themselves see ultra violet as a fourth primary colour, with which they are decorated in patterns unique to each individual. **WHERE** Wild budgerigars are widespread across most of mainland Australia. Flocks are usually small and nomadic, but the species' ability to take advantages of good conditions means that vast numbers sometimes converge in areas where water and food (flowering grasses) are plentiful, including irrigated farmland and reserves like Boolcoomatta and Bon Bon Station in South Australia.

© Edwin Remsberg | Alamy Stock Photo, © Martin Harvey | Alamy Stock Photo

Buffalo (Cape) *Syncerus caffer*

WHAT There's nothing tame about this distant relative of domestic cattle, widely regarded as one of the most dangerous and least predictable animals in Africa. Both sexes sport large horns which sometimes fuse at their base, forming a massive bony headpiece, known as a boss. It's a word worth bearing in mind if you find yourself wondering who's in charge during any encounter with this legendary animal. It certainly won't be you. **WHERE** African buffalo herds are a feature of forests and savannahs across much of sub-Saharan Africa. They need to drink at least daily so are seldom found far from reliable sources of water. Coincidentally, this brings them into contact with the only other animal capable of tackling an adult – the Nile crocodile.

Bumblebee *Bombus spp*

WHAT To bumble, verb: to move or act in an awkward or confused manner. It's a slightly unfair name for the endearing bumblebee, which although not the sprightliest of fliers, knows exactly what it wants: nectar from blooming flowers. There are 25 species of bumblebee in Britain, and almost a further 50 species in North America. But they're a very vulnerable species, beset by pesticides and habitat loss. Populations across the northern hemisphere are struggling, which is a cause for concern because these large fuzzy insects are important pollinators of plants. They live in small colonies in nests started by a queen every spring. **WHERE** Bumblebees are an essential part of the British summer – you'll find them in wildflower meadows and flower-filled gardens. In the southern counties of Kent and Sussex five rare varieties have made a recent comeback. Contact the Bumble Conservation Trust in the UK to find out how you can encourage bumblebees to colonise your area.

Burrowing owl
Athene cunicularia

WHAT The scientific name of this diminutive, diurnal owl commemorates Athena, the Greek goddess of wisdom. With eyes that seem to scrutinise your soul and find something to disapprove of, the analogy appears fitting. In fact, the forward-facing glare is an adaptation to stereoscopic vision and the studious tilting and swivelling of the head results from an inability to rotate the eyeballs. Despite their common name, burrowing owls rarely dig, preferring to adopt holes excavated by other animals. When threatened, they retreat to a burrow and mimic the warning hiss of a rattlesnake.

WHERE Burrowing owls are resident from the grasslands of Patagonia to Oregon, with summer breeding areas on prairies extending well into Canada. Several pairs nest on the Exhibition Grounds in Moose Jaw, Saskatchewan, where a Burrowing Owl Interpretive Centre is open from May to September.

California condor
Gymnogyps californianus

WHAT There is something truly special about the sight of a California condor in the wild. Not only is this New World vulture the largest bird in North America, with a wingspan of up to 3m, but the species' survival ranks as one of the greatest successes achieved by conservationists. In 1987, with the world population standing at just 27 birds, the last free-living individual was taken into captivity at San Diego Zoo and an intensive programme of breeding and reintroduction began. In 2016 the head count was 446, of which 276 live in the wild.

WHERE Rocky scrublands and forests of California, Arizona and Baja California in Mexico. Captive breeding continues at San Diego Zoo, where a small number of birds can also be seen up-close and personal.

California sea lion *Zalophus californianus*

WHAT Not all iconic wildlife is hard to find. Sea lions are masters of loafing, and watching them can be equally laidback. Alternatively you can don flippers and snorkel and join them in the water, where they are transformed into guided missiles of fish-seeking muscle. **WHERE** At the tourist hotspot of Fisherman's Wharf in San Francisco you can observe sea lions hauled out on pontoons while you enjoy a breakfast coffee and sourdough and they'll still be there as you sip a late-evening beer. The breeding range includes the length of the California and Baja California coast, but non-breeding animals are seen as far north as Alaska and south to Acapulco in Mexico.

Capercaillie
Tetrao urogallus

WHAT As spring sunshine warms the forested landscapes of northern Europe and western Central Asia, woodland glades echo with a sound sometimes likened to popping champagne corks, though the less romantic might find it more akin to glugging drains or a bout of hectic belching. This remarkable sound comes from a displaying male capercaillie 'lekking' in competitive display. He is a singularly impressive bird – resplendent in dark green and black, with a red eye-rose and a flamboyantly fanned tail. He is the largest member of the grouse family at up to 7kg, but his performance is aimed at a bird half his size and drably plumaged – the female.

WHERE Travel to the lake-studded wilderness of northeastern Finland in late April or May to encounter capercaillie on traditional lekking sites. There are good populations in Hossa and Oulanka National Parks and tours to see and photograph them operate out of the remote communities of Kuhmo and Kuusamo.

© Blickwinkel | Alamy Stock Photo

Capybara *Hydrochoerus hydrochaeris*

WHAT The world's largest rodent resembles a metre-long marmot with a solid, pig-like body, slim antelope-like legs and webbed paws. Capybara are semi-aquatic grazers that rely on safety in numbers to avoid predation by jaguars, puma, ocelot, caiman, anacondas and harpy eagles. Groups number from a handful to 100 or more, and threats are signalled by barking alarm calls, triggering the whole group to gallop to the relative safety of the water – or if in the water, to make a dash for the bank. **WHERE** Widespread in the tropical and subtropical forests of South America from Venezuela to the La Plata estuary in Argentina. Outside protected areas capybaras are also hunted by humans, making them wary, but in reserves such as Tambopata in Peru, Barba Azul in Bolivia and Rio Pilcomayo National Park in Argentina they are surprisingly easy to watch, especially from boats.

Caribou *Rangifer tarandus caribou*

WHAT At 5000km for a round trip, the annual migration of caribou (the North American subspecies of reindeer) is the longest migration of any land animal, and amounts to roughly half a million tonnes of meat on the move. The calving grounds they travel to lie so far north that not even large predators such as wolves, bears and coyotes follow, but the price for this security is high – the deer are plagued by flies intent on sucking blood or laying eggs directly in their skin – don't forget to pack insect repellent on this one. **WHERE** Caribou occur over a huge swathe of northern North America, but the most impressive opportunities to watch them are during migration. Specialist tours operate in Alaska and Nunavik in northern Québec.

Cassowary
Casuarius spp

WHAT A party of 1.8m-tall prehistoric throwbacks roams northern Queensland in Australia and New Guinea. Sporting a shaggy black coat, a rough, red neck and a domed helmet, they're potentially dangerous to anybody who crosses their path. The cassowary is a large flightless bird that bears an uncanny resemblance to dinosaurs such as the velociraptor thanks to a 12cm claw on each foot and a short temper. But formidable as these tropical rainforest dwellers might appear, they too are threatened by habitat loss and the motorcar. Suburbia is no place for such birds but the southern cassowary, the most numerous of the three species, has been spotted in people's gardens.

WHERE Better places to sight a cassowary in the wild include the Daintree and Cape Tribulation region north of Cairns in northern Queensland and around Mission Beach to the south of Cairns. The birds are most active at dawn and dusk.

Cheetah
Acinonyx jubatus

WHAT There's a fine balance to be struck between power and weight, and no animal demonstrates this better than the world's fastest sprinter, the cheetah. The small head, tiny waist and long legs give an impression of frailty, but those spotted shoulders and thighs comprise immense slabs of muscle, capable of hurtling the animal from 0-60mph (97km) in just three seconds. Fortunately, if you're after more than an exhibition of speed, like all big cats, cheetahs are inherently idle when not hunting, and typically rest in elevated positions where they can scan for lions or other threats.

WHERE Scrub forest and savannah from the Sahara to South Africa, including Kenya's Masai Mara National Reserve, Serengeti National Park in Tanzania, Etosha National Park in Namibia and the Kgalagadi Transfrontier Park on the South Africa-Botswana border. Asiatic cheetahs are restricted to central and northern Iran.

Chimpanzee
Pan troglodytes

WHAT As our other closest cousin, along with the bonobo, an encounter with wild chimpanzees is a lesson in humility in more ways than one. Not only is our shared ancestry obvious in a variety of physical and sociological traits, but touring in this kind of forest habitat is hard work, and you'll almost certainly feel inadequate as chimps and other primates travel above and around you with what feels like mocking ease.

WHERE Five subspecies of chimpanzee are known in the swathe of tropical forest running across Africa from Guinea and Senegal in the west to Uganda, Burundi and western Tanzania in the east. Perhaps the ultimate opportunity is on the edge of the species' range at Gombe Stream National Park in the Kigoma region of Tanzania, the area best known for the long-running chimpanzee study started by Jane Goodall in 1960, and which continues today.

Chinchilla *Chinchilla lanigera*

WHAT Famed and exploited for their beautifully soft, deep, smoky-grey fur, these South American mountain-dwelling rodents became endangered in the wild more than a century ago. These days the fur and pet trade is supplied mainly by captive bred animals, but the species' wild range remains limited. With 60 or more hairs sprouting from a single follicle, the coat provides insulation against the fiercest of cold winds and serves as effective camouflage on rocky slopes. Long-tailed chinchilla are most active at the beginning and end of the day.

WHERE The remaining wild chinchillas have their own protected area, Las Chinchillas National Reserve in Choapa Province, Chile. The terrain is steep and rocky, and the best chances of a sighting are to be had by taking one of the hiking trails to north-facing slopes where chinchillas bask in early morning sunshine.

© Fred Bruemmer | Getty Images

Christmas island crab *Gecarcoidea natalis*

WHAT Every spring, a red army materialises from the forests of Australia's Christmas Island. The unstoppable throng, some 50 million strong, marches up to 9km in a straight line, to the nearest stretch of shoreline. Here they mate and two weeks later, at the turn of high tide in the last quarter of the full moon, females enter the sea to release billions of larvae into the water. If you're visiting a month later, you might also witness a reciprocal journey made by tens of millions of tiny crablings. Islanders go to great lengths to help – closing roads and erecting barriers to funnel the crabs to safe crossing places. **WHERE** The Australian external territory of Christmas Island lies in the Indian Ocean, 350km south of Java. More than 60% of the island is designated as a National Park.

Cicada (periodical) *Magicicada spp*

WHAT It's early June in a leafy eastern US residential street and the earth is heaving as it disgorges a horde of inch-long, sap-eating bugs. The same is happening in nearby gardens, woodlands and parks – a million or more insects per acre. Their mass emergence overwhelms the appetites of potential predators and ensures a high overall survival rate for the few weeks it takes the adults to mate and lay eggs. They die in their multitudes and their like will not be seen again in the area for 13 or 17 years, depending on species. **WHERE** Periodical cicadas occur only in eastern North America, with 13-year broods dominating in the south, and 17-year broods in the northeast. Schedules for the various broods are available online and it's possible to plan a trip to coincide with an expected emergence in most years.

Clownfish (or anemone fish) *Amphiprioninae spp*

WHAT With their solemn faces and traffic-cone colours, these delightful reef-dwellers are popular with divers and snorkellers, and achieved wildlife megastardom with the release of Disney Pixar's *Finding Nemo*. When the thrill of meeting a global celebrity has subsided, you might notice how a coating of specialist slime permits clownfish to cruise among the stinging tentacles of large anemones, where they (and their eggs and offspring) are safe from predators. In return, the fish drive away potential parasites and predators of the anemone. They also consume leftovers from anemone meals, and nutrients from their droppings are absorbed by the host. **WHERE** Shallow reefs of the Indian and Pacific Oceans, including much of the Great Barrier Reef, Pulau Menjangan reef in Bali, Bamboo Island near Koh Phi Phi in Thailand and Ras Um Sid reef in the popular Red Sea resort of Sharm El Sheikh. All can be reached by snorkelling.

THE A-Z OF WILDLIFE WATCHING

Coelacanth
Latimeria spp

WHAT Eighty years ago, coelacanths were known only as fossils. But on finding something unusual in a trawl net in December 1938, Hendrik Goosen, the quick-thinking captain of a South African fishing vessel, called in local museum curator Marjorie Courtney-Latimer. The rest is zoological history; not only was the fish heralded as a living fossil, it also represents a crucial link between fish and tetrapod vertebrates (amphibians, reptiles, birds and mammals). Its fleshy fins resemble the legs on which our shared ancestor first hauled itself from the water. Coelacanths are deep-water specialists, but they may be encountered by divers or caught by fishermen.

WHERE Two species of living coelacanth are known, the steely blue *Latimeria chalumnae* from around the Comoro Islands, and the brown *L menadoensis*, from Indonesia. They are listed as Critically Endangered and Vulnerable respectively by the IUCN (International Union for Conservation of Nature), and any sightings should be reported.

© Mauritius Images GmbH | Alamy Stock Photo

Colugo (or flying lemur)
Galeopterus variegatus

WHAT The alternative name flying lemur is misleading, since this ghost of a mammal is not a primate and cannot fly. But it is able to travel up to 100m in a single shallow glide. The gliding membrane stretches from its neck to the tips of the fingers, toes and tail. By altering its posture in mid-air, the colugo can control the angle and direction of the glide and brake to reduce impact on landing. Glides are made between trees where the animals feed on leaves and other plant material. A colugo on the ground is virtually helpless. **WHERE** Colugos occur in forested parts of mainland Southeast Asia and the Malay archipelago. Bukit Timah Nature Reserve in Singapore offers good chances of a sighting. A second species occurs in the Philippines, but these are the only two representatives of an entire order of mammals.

Comb jelly *Phylum ctenophora*

WHAT You may have seen glow worms, admired the aurora, and surfed a phosphorescent tide, but here's another natural lightshow not to be missed. Comb jellies are non-stinging gelatinous creatures that differ so profoundly from all other life on Earth that the 150 or so known species are classified as a separate phylum. Their fringes (or combs) of tiny translucent hairs play tricks with visible light, resulting in exquisite flickering rainbows. All but the sea gooseberries (*Pleurobrachia spp*) are able to generate their own light, but even without bioluminescence the combs of sea gooseberries create a colourful lightshow using refracted daylight. **WHERE** Comb jellies occur in seas and oceans around the globe. Many species undergo daily and seasonal migrations during which they may form coastal swarms. These are unpredictable, so sightings rely on luck and an ability to recognise opportunities as they arise.

Conger eel (European)
Conger conger

WHAT The world's largest eel can grow to sizes thicker than a man's thigh and 1.5m to 3m in length. The largest are females, and individuals living in wrecks and reefs often become well-known to local dive communities. They are predatory, capable of swift strikes, armed with needle-sharp teeth, and worthy of immense respect. They also eat carrion, ripping chunks from larger food items by latching and thrashing with the full force of their muscular body. **WHERE** Congers occupy coastal waters of the northeastern Atlantic Ocean and the Baltic, North, Mediterranean and Black Seas from Norway to Senegal. When fully mature, they embark on a one-way migration to spawn in sub tropical waters around the Azores and the Sargasso Sea. Guided dives at An Dubh Sgeir off the Isle of Skye in Scotland take in a well-known eel haunt known as Conger Crevasse.

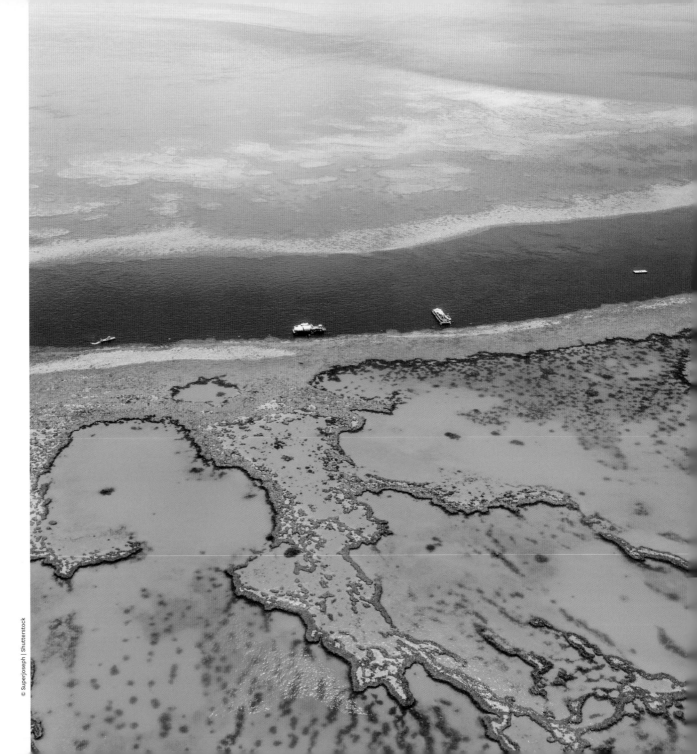

Coral
Anthozoa spp

WHAT Seeing a coral reef is, understandably, a regular fixture on many people's travel bucket list yet it remains hard to grasp the fact that corals are animals. Some of the 70,000 species of coral, which take an extraordinary range of forms, form symbiotic relationships with algae to build the largest living structures on the planet. In turn, ocean reefs have become rich habitats for a kaleidoscopic array of sea life. Each coral is made up of hundreds or thousands of invertebrates called polyps. Once year, corals in a reef spawn simultaneously (increasing the chances of fertilisation) and young corals attach themselves to the ocean floor. With the warming of the world's oceans, however, corals eject their algal collaborators and reefs become bleached.

WHERE The Great Barrier Reef (right) is the world's largest but Raja Amput in Indonesia is in immaculate condition. November to March offers the best visibility. You'll need to transfer via the city of Sorong from Jakarta.

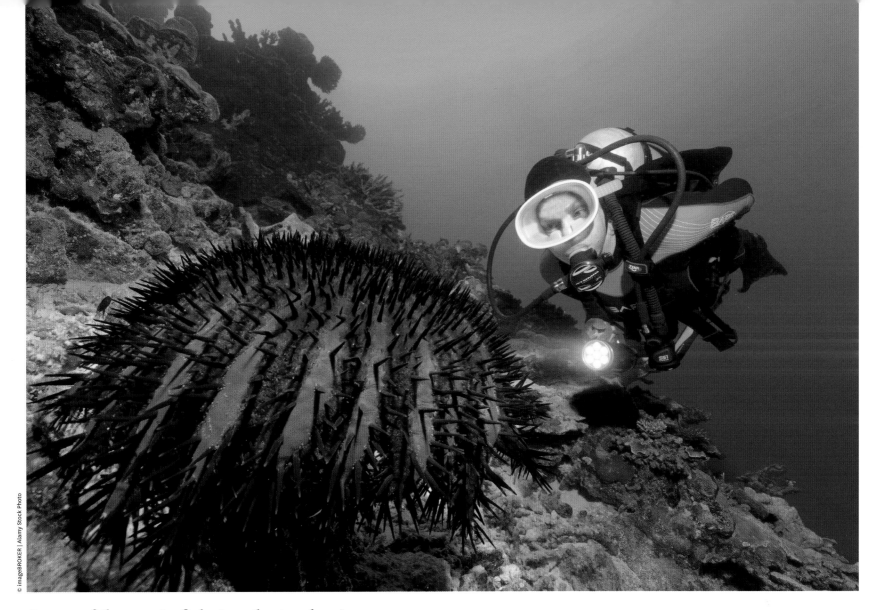

Crown of thorns starfish *Acanthaster planci*

WHAT This huge and distinctive animal achieved notoriety in the 1970s and '80s, when large increases in population were recorded on the Great Barrier Reef. They grow up to 1m in diameter and eat coral, sometimes at a much faster rate than it can regrow. While the hysteria surrounding the species has subsided, control measures continue to be enacted to relieve grazing pressure on the reef, which faces severe threats from climate change and pollution. Records of COT sightings can be submitted to the Great Barrier Reef National Park Authority using its Eye on the Reef smartphone app. Experienced divers are also recruited to carry out control, usually by injection of bile salts. **WHERE** The crown of thorns is widespread in the Indian and Pacific Oceans, but is thought to occur in greatest numbers in Australian waters, most notably on the Great Barrier Reef.

Darwin's finches *subfamily Geospizinae*

WHAT Among the giant tortoises, marine iguanas, great whales, penguins and frigate birds that make the Galapagos Islands unique live a collection of small and unassuming birds. While arguably not much to look at, a glimpse of any of these 15 black or brown birds carries special resonance for any naturalist. The Galapagos finches – or Darwin's finches, as they're often known – represent one of the best examples of how species form. Noting the consistent differences in the shape and size of beaks on birds from different islands, Charles Darwin realised they were all descendants of a common ancestor which had altered over time to the specific feeding opportunities on different islands. **WHERE** Fourteen of the recognised species live on one or more of the Galapagos Islands and nowhere else. The fifteenth member of the group is found only on Cocos Island, halfway between Galapagos and mainland Central America.

Dik-dik
Madoqua spp

WHAT Some animals are just plain cute. Take the dik-diks – perfectly formed antelopes in every way, elegant, leggy and alert. But adults are roughly the size of a domestic cat. Their elongated and flexible snout helps regulate temperature by accommodating large nostrils from which heat is vented. This extraordinary nozzle can also be wiggled to sniff in all directions. Dik-diks usually pair for life. Both sexes have small pointed horns, but these are rarely used in anger. Conflicts between rival males (distinguished by a punkish tuft of head hair) usually amount to nothing more violent than short dashes and bouts of emphatic nodding.

WHERE Four species of dik-dik occur across eastern and southwestern Africa from Ethiopia to Namibia and South Africa. Kenya's Masai Mara National Reserve and Samburu National Nature Reserve, and the vast Selous Game Reserve in south Tanzania all contain good populations.

Dingo
Canis dingo

WHAT Australia's red dogs are a cultural icon, but their ancestry is complicated. They probably arrived by boat from Southeast Asia between 12,000 and 3500 years ago, as semi-domestic companion animal descended from Tibetan wolves. At their peak they inhabited virtually the entire mainland, but were widely persecuted after the arrival of Europeans. Today, they are kept out of the southeast of the country by the 5600km-long Dingo Fence, constructed during the 1880s. **WHERE** The 200 or so dingoes that roam wild on Fraser Island off southern Queensland are among the most genetically pure in Australia, thanks to their separation from the modern domestic and feral dog breeds with which their mainland relatives have hybridised to varying extents. They can be seen all over the island, but make very sure you follow the 'dingo-safe' guidelines designed to keep dingoes and humans at a safe and mutually respectful distance.

© Matt Munro | Lonely Planet

Dinoflagellates
Dinoflagellata spp

WHAT Dino what? You may not have seen these creatures but you're likely to have heard of them. They're the single-celled bioluminescent plankton that can cause the sea in certain parts of the world to glow with an alien light at night. A couple of thousand species of dinoflagellate exist but not all are bioluminescent (only about 6%). Those that are need specific conditions – warm, still, shallow seawater – and are thought to react to disturbance with their flickering light. The light shows can be disrupted for months after hurricanes while the dinoflagellates recover but pollution is a bigger threat to this remarkable phenomena.

WHERE Mosquito Bay on the isle of Vieques off Puerto Rico's east coast has long been one of the brightest bioluminescent bays in the Caribbean (there are also bioluminescent bays in the Pacific). There are tours of Mosquito Bay. Vieques can be reached by plane from San Juan or by boat.

© Travelart | Alamy Stock Photo

Draco (gliding) lizard *Draco volans*

WHAT These feisty little dragon lizards are highly territorial, and battles between rival males are common. Usually these take place in the trees, and end with the vanquished individual being driven out along a branch. Sometimes he'll escape into a connecting tree, but if the branch is a dead end with nothing by empty space beyond he does what any dragon would do... opens his wings and flies. The 'wing' is a membrane stretched between elongated ribs; with wings extended and the tail switching back and forth as a rudder, the draco can make superhero glides of 60m or more to land safely on the ground or on another tree. **WHERE** Dracos are relatively widespread in forested regions of the Indian subcontinent and Southeast Asia, including Indonesia and the Philippines. Good populations exist in Tangkoko National Park in Indonesia's northern Sulawesi and Khao Sok National Park in southern Thailand, among others.

Duck-billed platypus *Ornithorhynchus anatinus*

WHAT Wait, is that a stick making those ripples in the river? It can't be, it just dived under the surface. It's near impossible to get a good view of a platypus in the wild yet this mammal is instantly recognisable: a small, sleek, brown-furred body with webbed feet, a tail borrowed from a beaver and, yes, a flat bill like a duck's. Seemingly composed from nature's spare-parts bin, it's a monotreme, meaning that it's a mammal that lays eggs and nurses its young on milk (see also the echidna). The voracious hunter uses its sensor-packed bill to follow the electrical signals of its prey, such as insect larvae and shellfish, along the bottoms of lakes and rivers. **WHERE** Most active at dawn and dusk, platypuses can often be found in eastern Australia's cleanest rivers and lakes. In the state of Victoria this includes Lake Elizabeth near Forrest and the Ovens River near Bright. Failing that, they're also housed at Healesville Sanctuary.

THE A-Z OF WILDLIFE WATCHING

Dugong
Dugong dugon

WHAT It's hard to see how the dugong could have been mistaken for a mermaid but that's how the story goes. Their closest relatives, however, are not fish-tailed women but elephants, which is almost as unexpected. However, they too are very large (up to 2.5m in length and 500kg in weight) herbivores that live in herds. Dugongs inhabit coastal seas around East Africa, the Indian Ocean and in the South Pacific as far as Australia (the manatee, a family member, lives in freshwater around the Americas). They graze at leisurely pace on underwater grasses. In fact, the dugong does almost everything slowly, including reproduction (about one calf per female every five years) and reaching maturity, meaning that their populations are vulnerable. **WHERE** Shark Bay Marine Park in Western Australia has large populations of dugong and is 400km north of Geraldton (which is a further 400km north of state capital Perth).

© Natalia Pryanishnikova | Alamy Stock Photo

Dung beetle
Scarabaeus spp

WHAT Of the many animal talents exhibited in this book, the ability of these scarab beetles to transport and bury 250 times their own body weight in excrement in one night ranks among the most industrious, not to mention ecologically useful. Balls of dung are used as a food reserve for the beetle's larvae. Remarkably, these are the only insects known to use the vast galactic sweep of the Milky Way as a navigational aid, and the only animals known to orient themselves using polarisation patterns in moonlight. **WHERE** Several hundred different species of scarab are known to collect animal dung and can be seen on all continents except Antarctica. Several species have been introduced to Australia as agricultural soil improvers. Members of the genus *Scarabaeus* are native to grasslands, farmlands and savannahs of Southern Europe, Africa and Asia.

Echidna
Tachyglossus aculeatus

WHAT Shambling through Australia's open forests, snuffling for ants, termites and other invertebrates, the short-beaked echidna is a relatively common sight but it never ceases to amaze. Firstly, its appearance is of a somewhat weathered creature, with rough quills poking through tawny fur and a long, narrow snout. But its lifestyle is more extraordinary: the echidna is an egg-laying mammal (like platypus). After mating (and that's a whole other weird process), the female lays a single egg, that hatches to reveal a bean-sized puggle, which feeds itself by lapping at a milk-secreting patch in the female's pouch.

WHERE Slow-moving echidnas often seem to have an absent-minded air as they forage for food on the forest floor but when they sense a threat they will wedge themselves into a hollow or hole. It's not a strategy that is much protection from dogs but it means that if you keep your eyes and ears open they're not hard to spot.

© Nicole Patience | Shutterstock

Edible dormouse *Glis glis*

WHAT In the days before canning or refrigeration, when fresh meat was difficult to store, an animal that self-fattened then went to sleep for six months, requiring no feeding or husbandry other than a cool dark place to hibernate, was bound to find itself in a larder. The Romans perfected the art of storing the torpid rodents in pottery jars, where their allegedly delicious meat could be kept fresh (ie alive) all winter. When awake they are noisy – listen for guttural churring from nest holes. **WHERE** Edible dormice live in forests of much of western and central Europe. There is a museum dedicated to the species (and the various traditions for hunting and eating it) at Snežnik Castle in Slovenia. A small introduced population lives around Tring in the English Chilterns.

THE A-Z OF WILDLIFE WATCHING

Egyptian plover (crocodile bird) *Pluviana aegyptius*

WHAT This unusual wader is a favourite with birdwatchers because of its striking markings and demonstrative behaviour. Paired birds greet one another at the nest site, usually on a sand bank close to water, by flashing black and white wing markings. In the absence of shade from the intense sun, parents soak their belly feathers in water to cool eggs and chicks, which they bury in sand while they are gone. Sadly there is no firm evidence to support the idea that the species cleans the teeth of crocodiles by pecking out morsels of food.

WHERE Gambia and Senegal are well set up for bird tourism, and this species is a speciality. Birds are usually present in Gambian coastal wetlands such as Kaur from October to January, when they move upriver and into the highland of Senegal. Niokolo-Koba National Park is an excellent place to see breeding birds.

Emperor penguin *Aptenodytes forsteri*

WHAT The first attempt to reach the Antarctic breeding area of emperor penguins in winter was immortalised in Apsley Cherry-Garrard's memoir *The Worst Journey in the World*, considered one of the greatest adventure travel books of all time. While that journey has become immeasurable easier in the intervening century, it is still a major undertaking, and for the penguins it ranks as one of the great feats of animal endurance. Fortunately by the Antarctic summer (November to January), the breeding grounds are in striking distance of open water (usually via helicopter) and there are chances to see parents and young on land and in their element at sea. **WHERE** Expeditions depart through the Austral summer for the colonies on the Weddell Sea such as Gould Bay and Snow Hill Island.

THE A-Z OF WILDLIFE WATCHING

Emu
Dromaius novaehollandiae

WHAT The world's second-tallest bird is as earthbound as its larger relative, the ostrich, and can run almost as swiftly. Both are members of the ratite family (with the kiwi and cassowary), which is a primitive group of Southern Hemisphere bird species. Aside from flightlessness, they also have in common a style of plumage that more closely resembles shaggy hair from a distance. In certain locations it's possible to get closer to a flock of emus when they're preoccupied with feeding on shoots and seeds, and familiar with people. Emus are most closely associated with Australia but they're also found on New Guinea and other South Pacific islands. **WHERE** Emus are widespread across Australia – keep an eye out when driving through grasslands. They tend to travel in large flocks. One reliable location for seeing emus is around Halls Gap in the Grampians National Park, 250km west of Melbourne.

© Colacat | Getty Images

Ethiopian wolf *Canis simensis*

WHAT The Ethiopian Highlands, considered the roof of Africa, are a biological lost world, with a large number of species found nowhere else on Earth. Perhaps the most iconic is the Ethiopian wolf. Though they rank among the world's most endangered carnivores, these handsome canids are respected by local people, and being less secretive than the grey wolf, they are rewarding to watch. Packs patrol territorial boundaries morning noon and night, and sleep in the open. **WHERE** Of a total adult population not exceeding 500, more than half the world's Ethiopian wolves live in Bale Mountains National Park, where the packs resident in Web Valley and on the Sanetti Plateau are closely studied by conservation biologists. They can sometimes be seen from the park's few roads, and seem largely to ignore passing vehicles. Further populations exist in the Arsi Mountains, Borena Saiynt Regional Park and Simien Mountains National Park, and in the community reserves of Menz-Guassa and Abuna Yosef.

European bison (wisent)
Bison bonasus

WHAT On misty mornings in the primeval treescape of Białowieża Forest, on the Poland-Belarus border, it's possible to glimpse a creature from another time. It's a wisent, or European bison, now the largest land mammal in Europe. You could be forgiven for thinking that bison were exclusive to North America. Indeed, for a time, the American bison was the only species surviving in a wild form, as these once common Pleistocene giants were hunted to extinction in the wild in 1927. The species survived as a captive population of fewer than 50 animals, from which today's population of about 4600 is descended. **WHERE** In addition to the original reintroduced population in Białowieża, free-ranging herds of wisent can now be seen in Russia, Slovakia, Lithuania, Belarus, Ukraine, Romania, Latvia, Kyrgyzstan and Germany, and semi-wild herds are established in Moldova, Spain, Denmark, Bulgaria and the Czech Republic.

© Mark Read | Lonely Planet

European goldfinch *Carduelis carduelis*

WHAT With their lurid carnival face masks and flickering white and gold wing bars, goldfinches are among the most striking small birds in Europe and Asia. Their lively squabbling behaviour make them a satisfying species to watch, especially in large flocks, which often form in winter around reliable sources of food such as clumps of thistle, teasel and burdock plants or feeders stocked with suitable small seeds. **WHERE** Goldfinches are native to Europe, western Asia and North Africa, but look out for introduced populations in parts of North and South America, Australia and New Zealand. The species' close association with thistles is behind its frequent cameo appearance in Christian art, where its presence foreshadows Christ's crown of thorns, so you might also do some goldfinch spotting in galleries and churches.

THE A-Z OF WILDLIFE WATCHING

European otter *Lutra lutra*

WHAT If you can't get to Monterey to spot sea otters (see p245), the standard Eurasian otter is much more common, widely distributed and almost as endearing. The sinuous mammals grow to about a metre in length. They hunt fish and amphibians in both sea water and fresh water and are an excellent indicator of the health of waterways. Having declined over the 20th century wild otters are recovering across Europe. They have inspired writers such as Gavin Maxwell and Henry Williamson, whose *Tarka the Otter* (published in 1927) describes the lives of otters in Devon. Within 30 years of its publication, the common otter had been hunted to near-extinction in southern England. But the tide has turned and the otter is back.

WHERE Otters have returned to the Taw and Torridge rivers in Devon and the Tarka Trail ushers you through their landscape. Otters are also regularly spotted on Scotland's west coast.

Fennec fox
Vulpes zerda

WHAT In perfecting the world's smallest canid, evolution has taken a cartoon approach, miniaturising everything except the eyes, and showing zero restraint on the ears. These outlandish appendages serve to locate prey such as insects and small vertebrates concealed below ground, and radiate excess heat. Add to this a repertoire of squeaky-toy vocalisations, yikkering, cooing, purring and high-pitched barks, and you have an animal to melt the hardest heart. Even their habits are appealing. Pairs mate for life and there's an absence of the glands that give other foxes their stink. And yet, fennec foxes are tough – surviving Saharan extremes of temperature and aridity by feeding on a variety of plant and animals and virtually never drinking water. **WHERE** North Africa and the Middle East. The fennec fox is the national animal of Algeria. The huge Sahelian reserve of Ouadi Rimé-Ouadi Achim in Chad is a species stronghold, and sightings are routine in the western deserts of Egypt, for example at the Dakhla Oasis.

Firefly *Photinus carolinus*

WHAT Take your seats as dusk settles on the heat of early June in the forests around Elkmont, Tennessee, for one of the best shows on Earth. It's a concert of sorts – an evening chorus of light. The performers are one of about 2000 species of firefly known worldwide. All are actually beetles, which use flashes of bioluminescence from a lantern organ in the abdomen to attract a mate. Different species use different colours and sequences of flashes in the same way that birds have characteristic songs. What makes *Photinus carolinus* special is its ability to coordinate individual performances so that males flash together, then pause so that they can see the fainter answering flashes from nearby females.

WHERE Tennessee, and North and South Carolina, including Congaree National Park in the latter and the Great Smoky Mountains National Park, straddling North Carolina and Tennessee.

Flamingo (lesser) *Phoeniconaias minor*

WHAT Flamingos feed by dipping their head upside down into the water and filtering out microscopic shrimps and algae, principally the blue green alga Spirulina, on which they are heavily dependent, and from which, counter-intuitively, they derive the pigments that give their plumage its characteristic pink colour. **WHERE** This smallest but most abundant species of flamingo is widespread across southern Africa, the African great lakes and Rift Valley, as well as extreme West Africa, Yemen and India, principally the western state of Gujarat. Greatest concentrations of birds are seen at breeding grounds on alkaline lakes such as Natron (Tanzania), the salt pans of Etosha National Park in Namibia, Makgadikgadi in Botswana and at Kamfers Dam in South Africa. Flamingo tourism may be an important factor in protecting some breeding areas' habitats from other kinds of development.

Flying fish *Cheilopogon pinnatibarbatus*

WHAT Around forty species of fish have developed this startling ability. 'Flights' are in fact extended glides in which the huge pectoral fins open out to serve as aerofoils. But it's the tail that does the work, thrashing the water like an outboard motor to generate the airspeed required to get the fish fully airborne. Under optimal conditions glides can extend for several hundred metres, and be relaunched by a few flicks of the tail without the fish falling back fully into the water. This dramatic ability is an adaptation to escape underwater predators, which lose track of their quarry during the aerial phase. **WHERE** Evening flying fish tours depart from Avalon harbour on California's Catalina Island (Santa Catalina), about 35km off Los Angeles. The main flying fish season runs from May to September, sea conditions permitting.

Flying fox (grey-headed) *Pteropus poliocephalus*

WHAT The largest of Australia's four varieties of flying fox, this mega-bat's territory extends from central Queensland down to southern Victoria. They roost in a large colonies ('camps') before flying out at sunset to feed on fruit (and pollinate trees in the process). With a 1m-wingspan, seeing a phalanx of these terrier-sized bats flapping silently overhead is a spellbinding experience. But their foraging habits have made them unpopular with farmers and their messy roosts in city centres mean that they're often moved on. **WHERE** Flying foxes are routinely seen in Brisbane, Sydney and Melbourne – in fact they've been known to set up home in city-centre botanical gardens. Generally they will roost in daytime within 20km of a regular food source. Just look up as the sun goes down to see their silhouettes against the night sky. They're also present up to 200km inland.

THE A-Z OF WILDLIFE WATCHING

Forest elephant *Loxodonta cyclotis*

WHAT It's not often that a new species of mammal is recognised scientifically, particularly a new elephant. It wasn't until 2010 that molecular techniques showed that African forest elephants were in fact a highly distinct species in their own right, separated from their savannah-dwelling cousin for two to five million years. There are significant physical differences to look for – the forest species is smaller (less than 2.5m tall) and darker than the plains elephant, has a hairier trunk, straighter tusks and, like the Asian elephant, an extra toenail on each foot, making five on the front feet and four on the back. **WHERE** Forest elephants are confined to a small part of West and Central Africa. Gabon has one of the larger populations, centred on Loango National Park. The pygmy elephants of the Congo Basin, many of which weigh less than a tonne, are a small variant of the species.

Fossa
Cryptoprocta ferox

WHAT Madagascar's largest predator is a long (up to 1.8m, half of which is tail), lithe, bronze-coloured mammal. It resembles a cat but is more closely related to the mongoose. Ultimately, having evolved in isolation on Madagascar for more than 20 million years, it's as unique as the island's lemurs, upon which it preys during the night and day (in addition to other small mammals, fish and insects). The animals are solitary for much of the year, mating only between October and December, and, it is thought, number around 5000, so encounters are rare. **WHERE** Fossas live in the upland forests of Madagascar, mainly to the west and the east. They are present in some protected areas such as Kirindy Forest and Ranomafana, Masaola and Ankarafantsika National Parks but sightings require patience and luck. International flights arrive at Antananarivo and flights tend to be expensive.

Frigatebird (magnificent)
Fregata magnificens

WHAT There's no mistaking a frigatebird in flight. It owes its highly distinctive silhouette to an exceptionally long wing (the largest in terms of area to bodyweight of any bird) and forked rudderlike tail. Outside the breeding season the birds spend weeks far out over the sea, feeding, bathing and preening on the wing and never alighting on the water, where they would rapidly become waterlogged. Food, mainly fish, is scooped from close to the sea's surface, or acquired by mugging other seabirds. At breeding colonies, males are distinguished by their scarlet gular sac, which they inflate to give reverberating calls. **WHERE** Southern tropical and sub-tropical areas of the western Atlantic and eastern Pacific Oceans, with breeding colonies on the coasts of Florida, Central and northern South America, Galapagos, Cape Verde and several Caribbean islands. The largest is at Codrington Lagoon on the small Caribbean island of Barbuda.

© Natphotos | Getty Images, © Ewen Bell | Lonely Planet

Frilled lizard *Chlamydosaurus kingii*

WHAT This metre-long dragon has elevated running away to a performance art. The eponymous frill is a flap of colourful skin that normally lies pleated against the neck, but can be opened into a huge ruff, supported by cartilaginous spines, when the animal is agitated by fear or aggression. The display is made more dramatic by a wide pink or yellow gape, and a habit of rearing onto two legs. The same bipedal posture is also used if the bluff fails and the lizard really needs to flee. **WHERE** Frilled lizards are common in wooded areas of northern Australia and southern New Guinea, where their mottled colouration serves as excellent camouflage. They are mostly arboreal but descend from trees to hunt and warm their bodies to an efficient operating temperature. In the Northern Territory's Casurina Coastal Reserve near Darwin they can be seen basking on roadsides in the morning.

THE A-Z OF WILDLIFE WATCHING

Galapagos tortoise *Chelonoidis sp and Aldabrachelys gigantea*

WHAT Giant tortoises were once widespread, but suffered drastically from overexploitation by humans. Now they live on in remote island localities, where isolation allowed the evolution of distinct types. In Galapagos, for example, about 15 species or subspecies are recognised, with those on arid islands smaller than their cousins and with a saddle-shaped carapace rather than a domed one. Five of these species are extinct, with the most recent loss in 2012 when the last Pinta Island tortoise, known as Lonesome George, died at the Charles Darwin Research Station on Santa Cruz. **WHERE** Galapagos giant tortoises live on seven islands, and specimens of several varieties can be seen at close quarters at the Fausto Llerena Tortoise Center on Santa Cruz. The main population of Aldabra giant tortoise can bee seen on the Aldabra Atoll in the Seychelles, with smaller populations on other islands in the archipelago, as well as on Mauritus and neaby Rodrigues, and Changuu Island off Zanzibar.

Gaur
Bos gaurus

WHAT The highland forests of India are home to the gaur, also known as the Indian bison. These hulking wild cattle are a similar size as the American bison but possess far larger horns. Males stand up to 2m tall at the shoulder and may weigh 1500kg. They're such formidable creatures that even Bengal tigers will tend to take only sick or young gaur. But it is listed as a vulnerable species, due to human encroachment on its habitat, meaning that family groups of gaur can sometimes be seen grazing through village gardens.

WHERE Several national parks in India have support populations of gaur and Bandipur National Park, lying along the temperate mountain forests of the Western Ghats in Karnataka state has about 2000 individuals – and a number of tigers and leopards. The nearest major city is Bangalore, about five hours' from the park.

Gecko
Gekkonidae spp

WHAT As any backpacker who has watched a gecko in their humid cabin or room knows, most of this numerous variety of lizard can climb walls and scurry across ceilings effortlessly, thanks to sticky toe pads fitted with *setae*, or very fine filaments that grip when directional pressure is applied. There are about 1500 species of gecko and one of the largest and loudest (both vocally and visually) is the tokay gecko (right) of south and southeast Asia. The tokay's natural habitat is forest, where it hunts insects at night, but it has become adapted to human habitation, like the much smaller common house gecko. Geckos in southeast Asia are generally viewed as good omens – or an ingredient of traditional medicine.

WHERE The tokay gecko is widely distributed, with colonies now established in Florida. But it is most likely spotted on its home turf of southeast Asia from Nepal to Vietnam (it is scarcer in the Philippines due to poaching).

© Blickwinkel / Alamy Stock Photo

Gelada
Theropithecus gelada

WHAT The grasslands of the Ethiopian Highlands are maintained by herds of grazers. Nothing unusual in that, maybe, except that some of the most conspicuous grass-eaters are not hooved animals or even rabbits, but baboon-like gelada monkeys, which graze by day and retreat to precipitous cliff ledges to sleep at night. Geladas society is hierarchical and complex, with groups interacting almost continually, so that grazing herds resemble a community picnic, rife with gossip, intrigue and the occasional brawl. The bare skin on the chest, flushed red in males and oestrus females, leads to the alternative name 'bleeding-heart' monkey.

WHERE Geladas are a highlight of the Simien Mountains National Park, which earns World Heritage Site status several times over, for its distinct landscape, culture and biodiversity. In effect the high plateaux are islands within which isolated species have undergone private evolution.

Giant anteater
Myrmecophaga tridactyla

WHAT It takes a lot of ants and termites to sustain a 1.8m-long animal – about 30,000 per day, which the giant anteater licks up with its 60cm tongue, having clawed its way into termite mounds and ant nests or demolished rotting logs with 10cm claws. Despite its size, half of which is a bushy tail at one end, and with a nozzle-shaped snout at the other, the solitary, shy and nocturnal giant anteater is an elusive creature to spot. It is thought that there are only about 5000 in the wild. **WHERE** The giant anteater has increasingly retreated from Central America so to see one you'll need to travel to Argentina, Bolivia or Brazil. The Pantanal wetlands of Brazil offer some of the best opportunities, for example around the Pousa Alegre ecotourism lodge in Mato Grosso. Rainfall is lowest from August to September when anteaters may seek out waterholes.

Giant clam
Tridacna gigas

WHAT The US Navy's diving manual during World War II gave instructions on how divers could release themselves from a giant clam's clasp by cutting its adductor muscle. But the advice was misplaced: there have been no recorded instances of humans being eaten by giant clams. Instead, these bivalve molluscs, up to 1.3m in length, actually nurture its own algal source of nutrition. Their beautiful folded shells are becoming a less regular sight along the coral reefs of the South Pacific and the Indian Ocean; once the clam has fastened itself to a location, there it stays for life. Spawning occurs according to lunar phases, with adult giant clams releasing 500 million eggs during their lifespan of up to a 100 years. **WHERE** Giant clams live along the Australia's Great Barrier Reef Marine Park, with scuba divers sighting some spectacular examples off Port Douglas.

Giant cuttlefish *Sepia apama*

WHAT The mastery of colour exhibited by the largest of all cuttlefish species is second to none. Not only are the pigment cells in its skin able to produce pretty much every colour in the visible spectrum, the layered arrangement of these cells has the effect of polarising reflected light, producing patterns which the animals are presumably able to see using their highly developed eyes. Giant cuttlefish are also able to change the texture of their skin, raising bumps and granules that allow them to mimic their surroundings with near-magical accuracy – the next best thing to an invisibility cloak. **WHERE** Coastal waters off southern Australia, from Shark Bay in the west and southern Queensland in the east, to beyond the southern tip of Tasmania. Several dive operators in Whyalla on the Spencer Gulf offer cuttlefish encounters.

Giant freshwater lobster *Astacopsis gouldi*

WHAT This fascinating and fearsomely clawed behemoth – clad in mottled green, brown and black armour – is the largest freshwater invertebrate in the world. The oldest specimens once exceeded 5kg in weight and 80cm in length, but today they rarely attain half that size. Females are much the larger gender and reach their breeding maturity at 14 years of age; they can live for up to 60 years. They're an integral part of Tasmania's ecosystem (the young are food for platypus) but are one of Australia's most threatened species. **WHERE** The giant freshwater crayfish dwells only in clean tannin-stained rivers and streams and still pools in the north of Tasmania, lurking beneath submerged logs and rocks. Endangered by habitat loss and sediment associated with logging, they survive mainly in the most remote regions of the island state, such as the Tarkine wilderness in the northwest corner of Tasmania.

Giant Gippsland earthworm
Megascolides australis

WHAT Yes it's a worm. An ordinary looking earthworm in pretty much every respect except one. These annulated beauties average about 1m long and some true monsters have been recorded at up to 3m. They burrow and feed in much the same way as regular earthworms, but their size means that their movements can sometimes be detected from above ground as audible squelches or gurgles. The giant worms are threatened, and conservation measures are in place, including encouraging farmers to switch from arable to livestock so that fewer worms die when fields are ploughed. Captive breeding has not yet been successful. **WHERE** They're found only in the damp clay soils of pastureland in Gippsland, Victoria. An eccentric museum dedicated to the species was forced to close in 2012 over licensing irregularities.

Giant millipede
Archispirostreptus gigas

WHAT For some the stuff of nightmares, for others a source of fascination: yes, people respond differently to the giant millipede. It can grow up to a third of a metre in length. And the $64m question, how many legs? Typically 200 to 300, depending on how many times it has moulted (they gain legs each time and can live for five to seven years). The giant millipede lives in the rainforests of East Africa, feeding on decaying fruit and vegetation on the forest. With no eyes (or indeed, a nose – they breathe through holes along their body), they use their antennae to navigate. Unlike centipedes, they can't bite people either.

WHERE Millipedes are most commonly sighted in tropical woodlands of East Africa (including Kenya, Mozambique and Tanzania), though they've also been found in Namibia and beyond. In Tanzania, try the national parks of the Udzungwa Mountains or Tarangire National Park near Arusha, Tanzania's capital.

Giant panda *Ailuropoda melanoleuca*

WHAT The image of a black and white bear has become synonymous with global conservation, and saving these iconic wholly vegetarian members of the order Carnivora is a matter of national and global pride, at almost any price. The task is huge given the species' famously restricted niche and apparent reluctance to breed, but no matter, to the Chinese they are animal royalty. **WHERE** The Chinese province of Sichuan boasts no fewer than 16 giant panda reserves and parks, mostly in the Qionglai and Jiajin Mountains. The city of Chengdu styles itself the panda capital of the world, with three panda conservation bases within striking distance at Bifengxia, Dujingyan and Gengda, where visitors in late summer or early autumn can see newborn cubs being reared for reintroduction to the wild. Treks to see pandas in the wild come with no guarantee of success, but also offer chances to see red panda and snow leopard.

Gibbon (white-handed)
Hylobates lar

WHAT Time your visit to rainforest retreats in Southeast Asia early, or stay overnight to be sure to hear the morning 'great call' – the far-carrying gibbon equivalent of a dawn chorus. The calls of white-handed or lar gibbons are melodious bubbling hoots, given by both males and females to reassert their family claim to a territory for the day. Like all gibbons, these are supreme brachiators – able to swing from tree to tree with startling speed and hang effortlessly from hands that form hooks without any muscular contraction.

WHERE Widespread but scattered populations of lar gibbons occur from Laos through Thailand, eastern Myanmar and the Malay peninsula to northern Sumatra, mainly in reserve areas such as Thailand's Khao Yai National Park. The species may be extinct in its Chinese range.

Giraffe *Giraffa camelopardalis*

WHAT The giraffe is an animal whose form is familiar to most from the cradle, and yet the real thing still surprises. The immensity of the neck is almost architectural. Those legs are not only long, but powerful. The eyes are huge, flirtatiously lashed and the tongue is a 46cm serpentine lasso. And the whole is an animal with grace and personality as well as stature. A genuine star of the savannahs. **WHERE** Giraffes in different areas of this vast range are genetically isolated and may constitute as many as nine different species, some of them severely threatened, but as yet there is no consensus on how to divide them up. Murchison Falls National Park in Uganda, Etosha in Namibia and Kruger in South Africa are bucking the species' declining trend with increasing populations, and at Kouré in Niger the critically endangered West African subspecies has increased tenfold in 20 years.

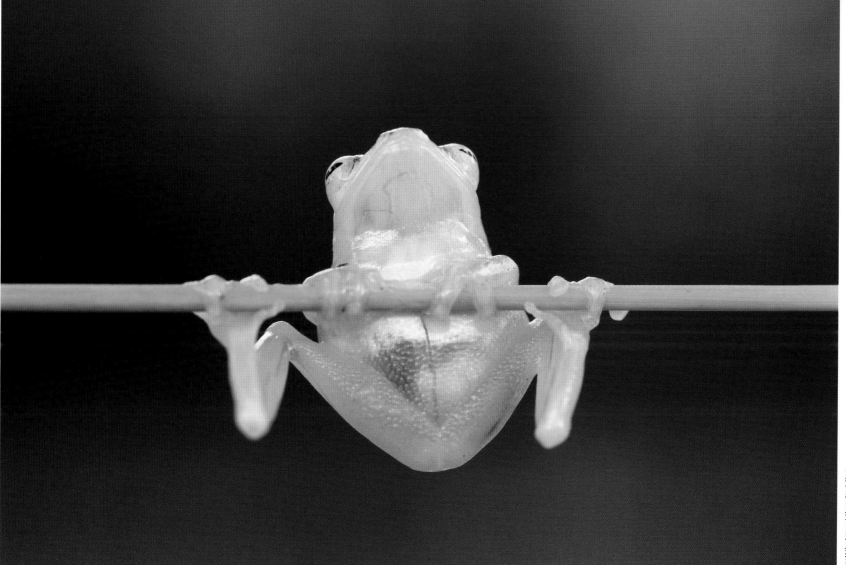

Glass frog *Hyalinobatrachium valerioi*

WHAT Eyes peeled. You're looking for a devoted parent with ninja kickboxing skills, but also a master of camouflage and only slightly bigger than a man's thumbnail. Glass frogs are tiny tree frogs whose transparent abdomen and disruptive colouring help break up their outline. Like all amphibians, they depend on water for at least part of their life history, but rather than spawning directly into streams or pools the female frog lays eggs on overhanging leaves from which the tadpoles drop upon hatching. This arrangement keeps the eggs safe from aquatic predators, but leaves them vulnerable to the attention of parasitic flies and wasps, so the male parent stays close by to protect his brood. **WHERE** Glass frogs of this and other species occur throughout the lowland rainforests of Colombia, Ecuador, Panama and Costa Rica. The private Mashpi Reserve near Quito in Ecuador boasts exceptional biodiversity, with amphibians a speciality.

Glowworm *Arachnocampa luminosa*

WHAT A nature tour of New Zealand would not be complete without a visit to one of the country's celebrated glowworm caves, and yet the extraordinary luminescent invertebrate responsible for the display is not actually a worm. Nor, like many other so-called glowworms occurring elsewhere in the world, is it a beetle. Meet what the Maoris call *titiwai*, the New Zealand fungus gnat. Both adults and larvae glow, the former to attract a mate, the latter to lure prey (mainly other small flying insects), which become tangled in sticky threads spun by the larva to snare them. **WHERE** The showcaves of Waitomo in North Island are the best-known and most widely promoted glowworm hotspot, but glowworms can be seen in other caves and sheltered areas of woodland all over New Zealand, bringing impromptu magic to evening excursions.

Golden eagle
Aquila chrysaetos

WHAT Present in North America, Europe, Asia and North Africa, the golden eagle is one of the world's most majestic birds of prey. Soaring above their expansive territories on wings almost 2m across, golden eagles watch for prey, ranging from small animals, such as rabbits and marmots, to the young of larger mammals and occasionally other birds. In winter and early spring the eagles court each other with acrobatic flights and may mate for life, often returning to the same nesting sites. Young are raised from April to September.

WHERE In Britain, the west of Scotland and the Scottish Highlands are its stronghold; the Isle of Harris has breeding pairs and an observatory. In North America, it can be found along the west of the continent, from Mexico to Alaska.

Golden lion tamarin
Leontopithecus rosalia

WHAT With as much as 98% of their Brazilian coastal cloud forest habitat lost, these conspicuously carroty marmosets are now restricted to tiny pockets of land surprisingly close to the megacity of Rio de Janeiro. They are highly arboreal, and unusually for monkeys, have sharp claws rather than flat nails, as an adaptation to climbing tree trunks. They live in lively territorial family groups and move unpredictably in search of food (mainly fruit and insects) by day, using high-pitched, birdlike calls to keep in touch.

WHERE Under strict protection tamarin numbers in the wild have increased from around 200 in the 1970s to 3500. About 1000 of these live within Poco des Antas Biological Reserve in Silva Jardim, a two-hour drive from Rio. Bear in mind that opening times are limited and visits, which take the form of a guided tour, must be booked at least a week in advance.

© Eric Gevaert | Alamy Stock Photo

Goliath bird-eating spider *Theraphosa blondi*

WHAT The largest tarantula you'll ever have the privilege to meet has attitude to match. When cornered it is likely to hiss violently and rear up to display fangs large enough to puncture human skin. The venom is no worse than that of a bee sting, but the fine 'urticating' hairs that can be forcibly ejected from the spider's body contain a nasty irritant – you really don't want one in your eye. But the name is hyperbole – bird-eaters very seldom eat birds. Their diet comprises mostly worms, insects and occasionally small lizards and mice. Despite the hype, they are routinely caught, cooked and eaten like shrimp by local children. **WHERE** Silk-lined nooks and crannies among rocks and tree roots serve as dens for the goliath bird-eater in the Adolpho Ducke Forest Reserve near Manaus in Brazil and in the rainforests of Venezuela, Peru, Guyana, French Guiana and Suriname.

THE A-Z OF WILDLIFE WATCHING

Grant's golden mole
Eremitalpa granti

WHAT The Namib desert is a shifting world, where sand sings and dunes moan. The few plants that maintain a roothold serve as oases of stability and sparse clumps of dune grass are well worth a closer look. Early in the morning, marks in the sand provide clues to the movements of one of Africa's more bizarre mammals. Golden moles have a cylindrical body and silky fur. Their eyes are completely overgrown with skin and their snout is covered by a tough pad. Short, powerful legs propel them through sand in a movement more like swimming than digging as they hunt prey including invertebrates and small lizards using sound, scent and vibration.

WHERE Grant's golden mole is restricted to South Africa and eastern Namibia – Namib-Naukluft National Park and the NamibRand Nature Reserve are a good bet. Other golden mole species occur across southern Africa.

© Minden Pictures | Alamy Stock Photo

Great bustard *Otis tarda*

WHAT Weighing in at around 15kg, male great bustards are the heaviest flying birds on earth. Understandably, they spend a lot of time foraging on the ground – preferring flat grasslands where their 1m height helps them look out for predators. Their size also made them a target for hunters and the last British bustard was shot in 1832. However, the bulky brown-and-white birds survived on mainland Europe and a small population was reintroduced to southwest England in 2004 and is now almost self-sustaining. The sight of a great bustard, with its wingspan of more than 2m, making a landing can thrill birdwatchers again. **WHERE** The British bustard population shares Salisbury Plain in Wiltshire with the British Army. The exact location is not publicised but it is possible to visit by contacting the Great Bustard Group to book a viewing. Bring your own binoculars.

THE A-Z OF WILDLIFE WATCHING

Great crested grebe *Podiceps cristatus*

WHAT This elegant waterbird inspired the theory of ritualisation, in which animal behaviourist Julian Huxley explained how actions can become exaggerated to serve purposes unrelated to their original function. In the great crested grebe, actions borrowed from preening and foraging behaviours have become part of an elaborate courtship, culminating in a finale where both male and female birds lift their bodies out of the water and dance vertically, with beaks full of waterweed. They hold position by frantic paddling of the legs, which are set near the rear of the body to maximise swimming speed. This arrangement makes the birds awkward on land, so they build floating nests immediately adjacent to open water.

WHERE Great crested grebes occupy well vegetated lowland lakes across parts of Europe, Asia, Africa and Australasia. To see them as Huxley did, visit Tring Reservoirs in Hertfordshire, England.

© Nature Picture Library | Alamy Stock Photo

Great hornbill *Buceros bicornis*

WHAT These strikingly robust birds grow over a metre long, and dominate the soundscape around regular roost with explosive 'roff' calls repeated at intervals of about a second. They disperse by day to feed – focusing mainly on fruit, but devouring small vertebrates they come across, typically by tossing them into the air and down the hatch like a peanut. The magnificent outgrowth of the male beak, known as a casque, is thought to function in sexual selection – which is to say it evolved for no other reason than females like them.

WHERE Great hornbills require large areas of old growth forest, and the expanding chain of National Parks and tiger reserves in the Himalayan foothills serves the species well. Regular roosts can be seen in Kaziranga, Pakke, Manas and Namdapha in north India, and in Anamali Tiger Reserve or Dandeli National Park in the Western Ghats.

THE A-Z OF WILDLIFE WATCHING

Great horned owl *Bubo virginianus*

WHAT In the depths of night in a snowbound Montana forest, an Arizona desert or the Brazilian Panatal, a rich, solemn call vibrates the air. Hu-hoo hoooo-hoo. The reply a couple of seconds later is slightly higher pitched: Hoo hu-hoo hoo-hooooo. The duet is between a pair of great horned owls. If you have a torch the light may pick up the ferocious butter-yellow glare of their eyes. In daylight you might follow the clicking calls used by smaller birds to mark the places where great horned owls roost. Look for the mobile feathery 'horns', which function in territorial and sexual communication, and if you want to impress your companions, use the magnificently precise term plumicorns. **WHERE** Great horned owls are widespread in North and South America, but for an encounter with spine-tingling resonance, head north, wrap up warm, step out after midnight into icy darkness, and follow your ears. The Owl Research Institute in Charlo, Montana offers field trips.

Great northern diver (common loon)
Gavia immer

WHAT The plumage of an adult loon is striking from a distance, but close up, it is a dazzling showcase of effects achieved with the simplest of binary palettes. There are areas of jet black and gleaming white. There are spots, stripes, bars, speckles, chequerboards, scales and blendings to soft gray. In marginal parts of the species range the appearance of such a spectacular bird causes a stir among birdwatchers, but they also retain iconic status in their core range. They are honoured as the state bird of both Minnesota and Ontario, and appear on the Canadian one-dollar 'loonie' coin.

WHERE Loons breed on lakes and quiet waterways throughout much of Canada and the northern US. Loon-watching cruises are commonplace and Loon Days and Loon-themed festivals are regular features in the local calendars of many communities.

Great white shark *Carcharodon carcharias*

WHAT Dur-duh... In the 40 years since a preposterous rubber shark erupted onto cinema screens and into a million nightmares, perceptions of 'Jaws' have shifted from terror to fascination, respect and even sympathy. Behavioural studies and GPS tagging mean we understand much more of what is going on behind those blank black eyes, and with understanding has come a level of predictability, commercial opportunity, and, for those who like their wildlife watching a little edgy, the underwater encounter of a lifetime.

WHERE South Africa dominates the white shark tourism market, with multiple operators offering cage dives around Dyer Island and Gansbaai in the Western Cape. Similar opportunities are available in the Spencer Gulf, South Australia, and off Guadeloupe. Always check codes of conduct regarding methods used to attract sharks. Excessive chumming and drag lures may teach sharks to target boats and people.

Greater kudu
Tragelaphus strepsiceros

WHAT A giant among antelope, male greater kudus stand at about 1.5m tall at their muscular shoulder, with their signature spiral horns extending another 1.5m. It is this impressive headgear that has made them a target for so-called trophy hunters but substantial populations exist in the national parks of Kenya, Botswana, Tanzania, South Africa and Namibia where they favour wooded grassland to the open plains. The tree cover – and their striped hide – gives them an opportunity to escape lions and wild dogs but also makes them more elusive for humans too – you'll get extra kudos for spotting a wild kudu.

WHERE Herds in South Africa's Kruger National Park prefer the wooded foothills and dense bush making access challenging. But in the more barren and arid landscapes of Namibia's Etosha National Park they're more likely to congregate around water holes among their less statuesque relatives.

Green sea turtle
Chelonia mydas

WHAT As adults, green turtles are exclusively vegetarian, and their diet of sea grasses means they are more coastal than other sea turtles, and easier to find. Until recently they were widely hunted for meat, oil and shell, and their name refers not to the colour of the skin or carapace but to the green-hued fat underlying the shell. A better name might be heart turtle, describing the shape of the carapace.

WHERE On the Greek island of Kefalonia, green turtles visit Argostoli harbour each morning as fishermen clean their nets. From May to October you can join beach patrols to record nesting efforts and sometimes observe hatchlings scrambling to the sea. On the Turks and Caicos island of Providenciales, you can pay a fee to help the local turtle conservation initiative catch and fit turtles with flipper tags or even satellite transmitters as part of ongoing ecological research.

© Doug Perrine | www.naturepl.com

Grey whale
Eschrichtius robustus

WHAT The migration of these blotchy giants between polar feeding areas and warm breeding waters is the longest of any mammal, at up to 22,000km for a round trip. They favour shallow waters and can thus be seen from land almost anywhere on their regular route down the western coast of North America. A smaller population in the western Pacific is showing signs of recovery too, and a handful of recent sightings suggest the species may soon become re-established in the Atlantic.

WHERE The grey whales that calve in the shallow coastal lagoons of Baja Mexico and the Gulf of California each January are local celebrities. Mothers and young are intensely curious, and while codes of conduct forbid active pursuit by whale watchers, the whales don't know that and readily approach small boats, nudging and occasionally even presenting a vast, barnacle-encrusted head for patting or splashing.

Grey wolf *Canis lupus*

WHAT Admired and reviled in equal measure, the ancestor of man's best friend has been eradicated from many developed areas of its once immense Eurasian and North American range, and continues to face persecution in the wild. But the 'Big Bad Wolf' is a keystone species without which populations of prey, especially deer, increase dramatically, with severe consequences at landscape scale. The ecology of these interactions is fascinating, but a close encounter with the species draws on something more visceral than science and reveals this social, intelligent and collaborative predator as our equal in more ways than one. **WHERE** The Lamar Valley in Yellowstone National Park was the site of a controversial reintroduction of wolves in 1995. This small but intensively studied population is celebrated for its spectacular contribution to ecosystem restoration, but relationships with local people remain conflicted.

Guanaco *Lama guanicoe*

WHAT It looks like llama, sounds like a llama and walks like a llama – but it's actually a guanaco, thought to be the wild descendent from which the llama was domesticated. Like the llama, it lives along the Andes and throughout the plains of South America. Charles Darwin described the guanaco as 'an elegant animal, with a long, slender neck and fine legs.' Being a camelid, it's able to survive in such arid environments as the Atacama desert. They're also comfortable at altitude, having extra-large hearts. About 7000 years ago they began to be domesticated by local tribes. To understand a guanaco, look at its ears: up means relaxed, forward signals alarm and flat is a sign of aggression. **WHERE** Patagonia is perfect guanaco habitat: visit Tierra del Fuego and the Torres del Paine National Park in Chile to find wild ones.

Hammerhead shark *Sphyrna mokarran*

WHAT The great hammerhead is one of ten shark species in which a strange head bears a bizarre-looking structure called the cephalofoil, which varies from a bonnet slightly wider than the rest of the body to the huge, square mallet of the great hammerhead. The shape increases the area of snout that can be covered with tiny sensory pits used by the shark to detect the electromagnetic pulses firing in the nerves of prey, and its hydrodynamic profile scythes the water, allowing this immense predator to turn with devastating speed and precision. **WHERE** Great hammerheads occur in tropical and warm temperate oceans and seas worldwide. Most sightings are in relatively shallow coastal waters but the species in known to be highly migratory, travelling into more temperate waters in summer. The island of Bimini in the Bahamas is a hammerhead hotspot from January to March.

Hanuman (grey) langur *Semnopithecus spp*

WHAT Named after a Hindu monkey god, Hanuman langurs are regarded as sacred in parts of their range, and get away with all kinds of misbehaviour as a result. These slim, silky-coated, dark-skinned monkeys were recently reclassified into seven species based in part on coat colour and the carriage of the tail. You can check this out for yourself if you're travelling around – you'll typically see tails curving forward towards the head in southern varieties and looping backwards in northern types. **WHERE** Grey langurs can be seen across much of India, where attitudes to their presence range from tolerance to ruthless persecution, based largely on the prevailing local religion. The temple of Galtaji in Jaipur is home to one of the most indulged troops, whose riotous behaviour is both an attraction and a nuisance.

THE A-Z OF WILDLIFE WATCHING

Hare *Lepus europaeus*

WHAT It's March in a downland field of southern England and a pair of male hares are leaping and boxing with each other. It's a sure sign that spring is on the way. The European hare is not native to the UK, having been introduced by the Romans, but it has become an icon of the English countryside, illustrated by 18th-century engraver Thomas Bewick and featured in Lewis Carroll's Alice in Wonderland. When not boxing in mating-season matches, the leggy, long-eared mammals are especially graceful and very well camouflaged against dun fields. **WHERE** Brown hares are widely distributed across England (mountain hares are residents of Scotland's uplands) but most easily spotted against open fields in early spring before grass and crops have grown. In the county of Suffolk, Havergate Island has a large population as does the island of Anglesey in North Wales. Also try the National Trust property of Uppark in the South Downs National Park, West Sussex.

© Robert Bannister | Alamy Stock Photo

Harpy eagle
Harpia harpyja

WHAT Monkeys scatter and shriek in terror as a huge dark shadow hurtles through the rainforest canopy. It's not after them, this time, but a three-toed sloth is less fortunate. Not a small animal by any measure – easily 5kg – it is killed instantly by the powerful and precise strike of the largest talons of any living bird, and carried away to be dismembered. Winged predators don't come any larger, or more spectacular than South America's harpy eagle, named for the hideous wind-spirits that bore the dead to Hades in Greek mythology.

WHERE Tambopata-Candamo Reserve Zone in Madre de Dios, Peru, boasts vast tracts of lowland rainforest habitat, and its mind-boggling biodiversity includes a bird species list longer than any similar-sized area on the planet – harpy eagles included

Hedgehog *Erinaceus europaeus*

WHAT 'The fox knows many things,' wrote the Greek poet Archilochus, 'But the hedgehog knows one big thing.' He was referring to the defensive ball of prickles that has served the species well in the 15 million or so years it has pottered about the planet virtually unchanged. Such is the hedgehog's faith in its 6000-strong spiny defence that it shows little fear and is one of very few wild mammals you can encounter literally nose to nose. Hedgehogs once thrived in woodland and low intensity farmland, but leafy suburbia may be the species' best hope in a changing world. **WHERE** Of all the places hedgehogs might be encountered across their huge Eurasian range, the one with most resonance might be the English Lake District, home to Beatrix Potter and one of the most famous hedgehogs of all, Mrs Tiggy-Winkle. Or, visit the Wildwood Trust in Kent, southern England.

Hellbender *Cryptobranchus alleganiensis*

WHAT Hellbender. Snot otter. Mud devil. The unkind names heaped on one of the world's largest salamanders belie the fact that this is a highly sensitive species, and its presence is generally regarded as cause for celebration among US ecologists – a sure sign of a healthy freshwater habitat. **WHERE** Hellbenders require clean, clear, swift-flowing, well oxygenated water, and stable rocky crevices in which to hide. The best remaining examples are to be found in the large National Forests of the Appalachian Mountains – such as Cherokee, Monongahela, Nantahala and Pisgah. Even here, hellbenders are well camouflaged and secretive, and finding them means searching underwater. So pack a mask and snorkel, move carefully, and try not to dislodge rocks that might shelter one of these extraordinary amphibians. August and September see peak activity as males begin wrestling for territories before females arrive to spawn.

THE A-Z OF WILDLIFE WATCHING

Helmet Vangas
Euryceros prevostii

WHAT A flutey descending trill shimmers the air in the rainforest cloaking the lower eastern slopes of Madagascar's northern highlands. The songster is a Madagascan speciality, the helmet vanga. Both males and females sport similar black body plumage with a foxy orange cape and tail, surprisingly inconspicuous in the dappled light and shade. But there's no mistaking that huge, startlingly blue bill, wildly over-engineered for the task of catching the beetles, crickets and butterflies that make up the vanga's diet. Almost as conspicuous is the pale yellow iris, which leaves you in no doubt that as you watch this bird, you are being scrutinised in return.

WHERE The best chances to see helmet vangas are in the remaining fragments of native rainforest within the northeastern Malagasy National and Natural Parks of Moarojejy, Makira, Masoala and Andasibe-Mantadia.

© Nature Picture Library | Alamy Stock Photo

Hercules beetle *Dynastes hercules*

WHAT With males exceeding 15cm, including their prodigious horns, this is the largest beetle on Earth. The horns are actually outgrowths of the exoskeleton – one sprouting from the head and a larger one from the pronotum, the shield-like covering of the thorax. The horns interlock with those of rival males during no-holds-barred territorial wrestling matches. The combatants have little to lose because even the most magnificent are short-lived, with less than six months in which to procreate. The larvae, which hatch and develop on a diet of dead wood, can weigh more than 100g. **WHERE** Costa Rica is a must on any entomological world tour. In Tortuguero National Park on the Caribbean coast, you stand a good chance of finding both the Hercules and the almost equally enormous elephant beetle. Search at ground level, in and around fallen dead wood.

THE A-Z OF WILDLIFE WATCHING

Highland cow *Bos taurus*

WHAT Scotland's shaggy-haired, huge-horned Highland cattle are not wild but they're such fun for visitors to spot in their Scottish homeland that they're included here. The cattle are a popular beef breed dating back to the 18th century, but records from the 6th century exist of Highland cattle. And scientists have discovered that they may be descended from ancient wild cattle, the aurochs. Despite their ancestry and appearance, they're relatively docile (although take care around cows with calves). **WHERE** Highland coos are farmed widely throughout Scotland. Queen Elizabeth II has a prize-winning herd (or 'fold') at her Scottish home, Balmoral Castle, which can be visited from April to August (daily). Or in the Scottish Highlands, try Rothiemurchus Estate, close to Aviemore, which offers a Hairy Coo Safari.

Hippopotamus *Hippopotamus amphibius*

WHAT Once celebrated for their fearlessness, hippos have become known in modern times as dangerously aggressive animals. Either way, they are worthy of enormous respect and best watched from a distance. They are aquatic, dozy and grumpily territorial by day, but businesslike at night, when they emerge to travel several miles to grazing areas.

WHERE The hippo's fearsome reputation means there are few places in their wide sub-Sarharan range where operators can offer safe close encounters. One exception is the Retina Pool in the Serengeti National Park, where viewers can approach on foot via the elevated and allegedly hippo-proof river bank. Bizarrely, there is also a growing colony of common hippos in and around Puerto Triunfo in north central Colombia – the result of escapes from a collection started by the infamous drug baron Pablo Escobar.

THE A-Z OF WILDLIFE WATCHING

Hoatzin *Opisthocomus hoazin*

WHAT The chicken-sized hoatzin is more weird than beautiful, belonging to a group that separated from other birds soon after the extinction of the dinosaurs. Biologically it is unique, having fermenting foregut digestion like that found in ruminants, and chicks have two claws on each wing that allow them to clamber around the branches of their nest tree. In all movements they appear clumsy and crash landings are routine. Indeed, they often seem unwilling to even attempt flight, and thus, once located, can be easy to watch. **WHERE** Hoatzins are widespread across the Amazon and Orinoco basins and on the Atlantic coasts of Guyana, Surinam, French Guiana and north Brazil. They inhabit waterside forests and can be watched from boats, as in Ecuador's Napo River or the mangroves of Mahaica estuary in Guyana, where they're the national bird.

Honey badger
Mellivora capensis

WHAT The honey badger's reputation precedes it: the master of mayhem, a fearless and frighteningly intelligent member of mustelid (weasel) family. Much of the honey badger mythology is true: they have been observed standing their ground against lions and they do have a taste for honey, although as unfussy omnivores they will try to eat almost anything. The two-tone creatures grow to about 75cm in length and 25cm at the shoulder and have a thick rubbery skin that is loose enough for them to turn around inside it. Widely distributed throughout sub-Saharan Africa (and the Middle East and the Indian peninsula) they're hard to find, being solitary characters (perhaps in part due to their no-nonsense personalities).

WHERE Honey badgers have been studied in the Kgalagadi Transfrontier Park in the very northwest of South Africa and western Botswana. The park is best reached via Cape Town and offers accommodation in several tented camps and some lodges.

© Johan Swanepoel | Alamy Stock Photo

Honey possum *Tarsipes rostratus*

WHAT This tiny marsupial is neither possum nor honey eater. But uniquely among mammals it is wholly dependent on nectar as a food source – sipping up to its own body weight every day. It feeds like a hummingbird, flickering a long, brushlike tongue into flower after flower – and performing an essential pollination service as it goes. Honey possums are largely nocturnal, but will emerge to top up energy reserves by day during cooler spells of weather. And, for the record, they have the unlikely double distinction of producing the smallest babies of any mammal (0.005g at birth) and the longest sperm (0.35mm). **WHERE** The southwestern corner of Western Australia is one of the few places in the world with the climate and year-round floral diversity to sustain a nectar-feeding, non-hibernating mammal. The rich banksia woodlands and heaths of Fitzgerald River and Stirling Range National Parks offer excellent habitat

Horseshoe crab
Limulus polyphemus

WHAT Every year on the eastern seaboard of the US, a spectacle worthy of a big-budget alien movie takes place. But there's nothing computer-generated about this armoured swarm. Not only are horseshoe crabs real, they have been performing this epic breeding invasion for 450 million years.

WHERE Horseshoe crabs come ashore on suitable beaches in May and June, with greatest numbers recorded in Delaware Bay. Visit on evenings with high tides, a day or two either side of the full and new moon. Known hotspots on the bay include Pickering Beach, Kitts Hummock, Pierce's Point beach and Slaughter Beach, which is managed as a sanctuary for the species. The mass spawning attracts flocks of wading birds so vast it's a wonder any eggs survive. But with each female producing between 60,000 and 120,000 eggs, the small proportion that makes it is ample to sustain the population.

Howler monkey
Alouatta caray

WHAT Few mammals advertise their presence more effectively than these surprisingly small primates. More of a roar than a howl, the territorial vocalisations of male howler monkeys come from a voicebox reinforced by an extra-large hyoid bone, and with amplification from the vibration of a large throat pouch. The result is one of the loudest animals sounds on the planet – audible for up to three miles and easily topping levels at which most health and safety laws require ear defenders.
WHERE At the Community Baboon Sanctuary in Belize, local landowners have pledged to manage their land for the benefit of their noisy neighbours. The result is more than 20 sq miles of accessible forest where wild black howlers (known locally as baboons) can be encountered at close range.

© Justin Foulkes | Lonely Planet

Humboldt squid *Dosidicus gigas*

WHAT Not quite the world's largest invertebrate (the very rarely recorded giant and colossal squids are considerably larger), but at up to 2.5m not including tentacles, the Humboldt squid is the largest to be seen regularly in surface waters, which it usually visits at night. These highly intelligent predators have a reputation for aggression, especially when hunting. The species uses bioluminescent flashes as a form of communication, and lights or reflective dive equipment may explain some documented attacks on people. **WHERE** The Humboldt Current brings cold, nutrient-rich water to the west coast of South America, feeding one of the richest open ocean ecosystems in the world. Humboldt squid are increasingly encountered well north of the current itself – even in waters off British Columbia and Alaska. Some dive operators in the Sea of Cortez offer nighttime squid dives for the bold.

Humpback whale
Megaptera novaeangliae

WHAT Make way for an all-singing, all-dancing global marine megastar. By far the most acrobatic of the great whales, a breaching adult humpback is 30 tonnes of exuberance, while a singing male offers a sound so mesmeric and melancholy that sales of humpback music rival those of many successful human artists. The species favours coastal waters, accessible to day-tripping whale watchers, whose interest often appears to be reciprocated by whales, which often venture close enough to share eye contact and a blast of eyewateringly fishy breath. **WHERE** Fifty years since the moratorium on hunting humpbacks, populations are increasing steadily in all oceans. In Hervey Bay, Australia, known individuals visit each year on migration and underwater microphones are deployed from tour boats to pick up their songs. To feel really small, try watching from a kayak in Hawaii, Alaska or the Saguenay-St Lawrence Marine Park, Québec.

© Georgette Douwma | www.naturepl.com

Humuhumunukunukuāpua-a (reef triggerfish) *Rhinecanthus rectangulus*

WHAT This feisty little reef dweller is the state fish of Hawaii. It has an English name, but its local title is way too much fun not to use (it can be shortened to humuhumu if you're in a hurry), as is its meaning: 'fish that grunts like a pig'. The grunts serve as an alarm call and are clearly audible as the fish scud away from a disturbance. The colours vary, not only between individuals, but over time – fading when the fish is resting or in poor condition as a result of changing hormone levels. **WHERE** Humuhumus are a small part of the abundant marine life that can be seen during snorkelling sessions on the reefs around Hawaii.

Hyacinth macaw
Anodorhynchus hyacinthinus

WHAT A metre long, and with an intensity of colour suggesting it is trying to compensate unilaterally for the scarcity of blue elsewhere in the animal kingdom, the hyacinth macaw is the big, bold, beautiful emperor of parrots. Recovering from severe endangerment in the 1980s, it is the subject of considerable research interest and a must-see for bird enthusiasts visiting South America.

WHERE Bolivia is the place to see macaws generally, with 12 native species to tick off, including hyacinths. But the largest numbers are over the border in the palm-tufted swamps of the Brazilian Pantanal. The species features prominently on wildlife tour itineraries, including those visiting the Caiman Ecological Refuge near Miranda in Mato Grosso do Sul, home to the Hyacinth Macaw Project, where tours are lead by researchers.

Indian rhino
Rhinoceros unicornis

WHAT The towering grasses and wetlands of the Ganges plain are a wilderness of suitably epic proportions for a beast that might have shoved its way out of a medieval bestiary, its armoured knobbliness a striking contrast to the leathery but smooth skin of its African cousins. And given its impressive bulk, it's amazing how close you can be to an Indian rhino and not know it...until it decides to charge, then it's best if you can move faster than the 50kph it can clock up over short distances.

WHERE Kaziranga National Park in Assam, northeast India is home to about 2400 Indian rhinos, about 70% of the world population, protected from poaching by armed guards. Rhino tourism is seen as a positive factor, attaching economic value to keeping the animals alive.

Indri *Indri indri*

WHAT It's morning in eastern Madagascar and the forest echoes with air-shattering wails the volume and pitch of an ambulance siren. Each burst lasts two or three minutes, and as it fades, a reply comes from another direction. Family groups of indri, or babakoto as they are known locally, are singing to each other. The Malagasy name means 'ancestor' or 'father of sons', and the upright stance, owlish stare and lightness of indri movement make it easy to feel kinship with this large, almost tailless lemur – just a few branches away from us on our shared primate family tree. **WHERE** Indri have never been successfully kept in captivity, but hunting and catastrophic shrinkage of their habitat threaten them with extinction in a few decades. Revenue from wildlife tourism may play a part in saving this extraordinary species.

Ivory-billed woodpecker *Campephilus principalis*

WHAT It has to be said that an expedition in search of what is sometimes called the 'Elvis bird' is the longest of long shots – the last confirmed sighting of a live ivory-billed woodpecker was in 1944. But, the hope that some survive has not gone away, and occasional reported sightings, blurry video clips and sound recordings have proved sufficient to keep its official status at Critically Endangered, rather than Extinct. Some of these records are almost certainly cases of mistaken identity of smaller pileated woodpecker, but others...well, it's not impossible. **WHERE** Most ivory-bill seekers focus on the species' last known stronghold in the swamp forests of Louisiana and Florida. Others have taken the search to eastern Cuba, where further tracts of suitable habitat exist.

Jacana (lily trotter)
Jacana jacana

WHAT The wattled jacana is a common and widespread wetland bird in South America, and not a challenge to spot. Like other jacanas, it is sometimes referred to as the Jesus bird; spend a few minutes observing them and you'll find out why as you watch their signature 'walking on water' behaviour. In the breeding season look for male birds sitting on nests of floating vegetation, while in a reversal of usual roles, their mates patrol the breeding territory, aggressively repelling other females. **WHERE** The Costanera Sur Ecological Reserve in Buenos Aires has a reputation for some of the best urban birdwatching in the world. The site developed naturally following the abandonment of a massive state construction project on wetlands alongside the La Plata River. Jacanas are among almost 300 bird species recorded here – look too for the oven-like nests of the *rufous hornero*, Argentina's national bird.

Jaguar
Panthera onca

WHAT South America's big cat is the poor relation to its African and Asian relatives in terms of publicity, but third only to tiger and lion in size, and arguably more powerful than either. While most cats kill with a suffocating grip on the throat or a surgical severing of the spinal cord, this matchlessly muscular carnivore simply delivers a crushing bite to the head – a tactic that works equally well applied to a wide range of vertebrate skulls or the heavy-duty shell of a large turtle. **WHERE** Perhaps the ultimate exhibition of jaguar supremacy is seen in attacks on another feared predator, the black caiman. For a chance to witness such a battle – or to see jaguars hunt any one of more than 80 known prey species, head to South America's northern Pantanal, where specialist guides offer tours of jaguar hotspots such as the Taiamã Reserve.

Japanese macaque *Macaca fuscata*

WHAT Humans aside, these stump-tailed, shaggy coated monkeys are by far the most northerly dwelling wild primates, able to survive winter temperatures as low as -20°C. They are the inspiration for the mystic wise monkeys who sought to see no evil, hear no evil, speak no evil. **WHERE** Japanese macaques occur on the main islands of Honshu, Shikoku and Kyushu and several smaller islands. Those living in Joshinetsu National Park are famous for bathing in hot springs during winter, while members of the troop on Koshima Island off Kyushu wash their food in a small stream running down a beach and dip clean food in seawater to season it – the first scientifically documented cases of culturally transmitted non-human behaviour and of animals choosing to alter the flavour of their food.

Kakapo *Strigops habroptila*

WHAT In 1995, just 51 kakapo survived. New Zealand faced a big choice: give up on this large, nocturnal parrot or try to save it. The Department of Conservation decided to not let this ground-dwelling bird go the way of the dodo. The Kakapo Recovery Programme established breeding populations on three predator-free islands: Codfish, Anchor and Little Barrier. In 2016, New Zealand's kakapo enjoyed a record year with 33 chicks fledging on their island sanctuaries. Things happen slowly in the world of the kakapo (they can live for 60 years and don't breed until they're five years old) but the hope is that this wonderful bird will recover. **WHERE** The public is not permitted to enter kakapo habitats. But you can follow Sirocco, a charismatic ambassador for the species on Twitter: @Spokesbird.

THE A-Z OF WILDLIFE WATCHING

Kea *Nestor notabilis*

WHAT With imported predators such as cats, rats, stoats and possums, New Zealand's unique ground-nesting birds have had a rough deal over the last century or two. The kea, the world's only alpine parrot, is one such bird and despite its evident intelligence and ingenuity – the mischief-making parrots have been observed turning on taps and using tools – are increasingly endangered by predation. There are thought to be about 5000 remaining in the wild but hikers in the South Island's national parks are quite likely to encounter trouble makers as they often frequent car parks to tear out the rubber linings for fun (they also eat berries, seeds, leaves and grubs). **WHERE** Kea live only at higher altitudes on New Zealand's South Island. One place offering regular sightings is Arthur's Pass National Park, deep in the New Zealand Alps, especially along Scotts Track to Avalanche Peak.

© Sharon Davis | Alamy Stock Photo

Keel-billed toucan
Ramphastos sulfuratus

WHAT This clownish bird is invariably seen in groups, often representing an extended family. They feed and roost together, flying as little as possible, but indulging in playful duels and games involving throwing and catching items of food from one outlandish bill to another. The bill is lighter than it looks, its bony substructure riddled with holes like a sponge, and the toucan uses it with surprising dexterity and delicacy to gather fruit and insect food, which is then manoeuvred into the gullet with a toss of the head. **WHERE** Keelbills occur from southern Mexico to northern Colombia and Venezuela. The species is the national bird of Belize, where it can be seen both on the mainland and on barrier reef islands such as Ambergris Caye.

Kinkajou *Potos flavus*

WHAT The dexterity of its front paws, and the ease with which it traverses the canopy using its prehensile tail as a fifth limb are monkeylike, and the nocturnal kinkajou fills the ecological niche occupied in daylight by spider monkeys. However, this agile fruit-eater is not a primate, but a carnivore from the same family as raccoons and coatis.

WHERE The adaptable kinkajou favours dense, close canopy forests including tropical rainforest, dry forest and secondary growth, from southern Mexico to Amazonia. The colossal UNESCO Maya Biosphere Reserve of northern Guatemala contains one of the largest tracts of natural forest in MesoAmerica, some of it National Park, but much of it community-owned and harvested sustainably. Kinkajous are among the diverse forest wildlife to benefit and are relatively plentiful, but you'll need to take a nighttime excursion to see them.

Kitti's hog-nosed bat
Craseonycteris thonglongyai

WHAT Also known as the bumblebee bat on account of its size, this tiny, pig-faced scrap of thistledown fur and wing vies for the title of world's smallest mammal (at 2g in weight and around 3cm long it is fractionally heavier but shorter-bodied than its rival the Estruscan shrew).

WHERE Kitti's hog-nosed bat was discovered in 1974 in a series of limestone caves in the Tenasserim Hills in western Thailand, and larger populations were later found in eastern Myanmar. Like all cave wildlife, it is highly susceptible to disturbance and conservationists advise that enthusiasts wishing to see this and other bats should resist invitations to visit small 'show caves' where any human activity is likely to impact on the microclimate. Large, established show caves are less of a risk, but better still is to wait outside to see the bats on their own terms as they emerge at dusk.

Knot (red knot)
Calidris canutus

WHAT Seen singly, this small, dumpy wader is an appealing but unspectacular bird. But knot are seldom alone, least of all during their extended spring and autumn migrations, when immense flocks constitute one of the great spectacles of bird numbers.

WHERE Knot breed in the Arctic, but for knot-watchers, the biggest thrills are to be had at migration stop-off points or wintering areas. There are designated knot-watching spots scattered along the coast of Delaware Bay in New Jersey, where flocks arrive for a few weeks from mid-May. In the UK, the huge estuarine expanse of The Wash hosts hundreds of thousands of birds in winter. At the RSPB reserve at Snettisham in Norfolk, knot pack onto shingle banks 200 to a square metre during very high tides, then whirl away like smoke as the tide recedes and feeding areas are exposed. Visit from December to March to see greatest numbers.

Koala *Phascolarctos cinereus*

WHAT Button eyes, a squashy-looking swatch of black nose, and contenders for world's fluffiest ears – with these teddy-bear features it's easy to see why the moniker 'koala bear' has stuck, despite the fact that this is really a kind of tree wombat. Once you've found them, koalas are an easy, if neck-straining watch, as their extreme low-energy lifestyle means they sleep 20 hours a day wedged in the fork of a tree. That large head contains a lot of shock-absorbing fluid in case of a tumble, and one of the smallest brains of any mammal relative to body size – another energy-saving measure. **WHERE** Koalas are widespread and relatively common in areas of suitable habitats throughout much of eastern Australia, so it's worth checking out groves of eucalyptus anywhere from Townsville, Queensland to southern Victoria and South Australia. Many reserves offer pretty much guaranteed sightings – for example You Yangs Regional Park near Geelong, Victoria and most tours of Kangaroo Island, South Australia.

THE A-Z OF WILDLIFE WATCHING

© aumphotography | Getty Images

© Guenter Guni | Getty Images

Komodo dragon *Varanus komodoensis*

WHAT This prehistoric, swaggering predator is the world's largest lizard and one of the few species in this book you might legitimately fear. Komodo dragons specialise in a slow and brutal kind of lethality. Once bitten, prey may take hours or days to die, with their nemesis in relentless, plodding pursuit. Up close (several metres is plenty close enough) you'll see the distinctive chainmail scales, a forked tongue sampling the air to detect the scent of rotting flesh from up to 5km away, and gooey strands of toxic saliva trailing from a mouth full of filthy, saw-edged teeth. Sweet dreams after a sighting are not guaranteed. **WHERE** Of the scatter of volcanic islands in Indonesia's Komodo National Park and Unesco World Heritage site, two (Komodo and Rinca) have dragons – about 6000 in total. An experienced guide is essential in order to encounter these thrillingly unpredictable reptiles safely.

Lammergeier
Gypaetus barbatus

WHAT The lammergeier (or bearded vulture) is unique in subsisting almost entirely on a diet of bones, which it smashes by dropping from great heights to access the nutritious marrow. This strategy is less mucky than feeding from fleshy carcasses, and allows the birds to retain the head feathers that most other vultures lack. Lammergeiers usually depend on predators such as wolves and eagles to provide food, though increasingly they also scavenge human refuse. Also helpful, given the species' immense size, are steep-sided mountains, where reliable strong updrafts help to keep the birds airborne.

WHERE These handsome vultures occur from southern Europe to central China and south along the Great Rift Valley. The population in Spain is increasing, aided by a burgeoning wildlife tourism industry that encourages conservation. In Ordesa and Monte Perdido National Park in the Catalonian Pyrenees lammergeiers are often seen alongside similarly impressive (but less beardy) griffon vultures.

Leadbeater's possum *Gymnobelideus leadbeateri*

WHAT Leadbeater's possums inhabit only a tiny patch of mountain ash forest in Victoria's Central Highlands. They're picky about their home and only nest in large, old hollow trees (mountain ash are among the world's tallest trees). The small marsupials – measuring about 30cm in length – were thought extinct until rediscovered in 1961 near Marysville. Logging has long been a threat to their habitat but it was the Black Saturday bushfire of 2009 that destroyed almost half of their forest range (and Marysville). Now thought to number no more than 1500 animals, captive breeding programs have failed so the focus is on conserving the possum's habitat with a campaign to create Great Forest National Park. **WHERE** While the overall territory of the critically endangered leadbeater's possum is known, specific nesting locations are not publicised so chance encounters in the wild are extremely unlikely (although that's no reason not to explore the mountain ash forests around Warburton, northeast of Melbourne). Healesville Sanctuary has some captive animals.

Leafy sea dragon *Phycodurus eques*

WHAT This exquisite, eccentric fish is an easy watch for divers and snorkellers, once you've located one. The seaweed-like lobes of skin for which the species is named provide remarkable camouflage, allowing it to avoid the attention of both predators and prey. It drifts about, relying on the shelter of kelp beds to avoid being swept away by even moderate currents, all the while sucking up tiny crustacean prey with its nozzle-like mouth. Bony skin plates keep the body rather inflexible and all the propulsion for swimming comes from undulations of the delicate, near-transparent dorsal fin. **WHERE** Leafies' are found only on southern and extreme southwestern coasts of Australia. A local dive guide will boost your chances of a sighting and several operators run tours off the Yorke Peninsula, Rapid Bay, Victor Harbour and other sites around Adelaide.

Leatherback turtle
Dermochelys coriacea

WHAT While most turtles have a bony carapace covered with horny plates (scutes), the unique leatherback has a covering of tough skin embedded with tiny bony growths. The ridged, teardrop-shaped body is hydrodynamic and the flippers are the largest of any turtle, relative to body size. Thus, while its usual swimming speed is a leisurely 8km an hour or less, the species is capable of bouts of over 32kph, making it one of world's swiftest reptiles.

WHERE Thanks to an elevated body temperature maintained by exercise, leatherbacks cope with surprisingly cool water, wandering as far north as Alaska and Scandinavia, and further south than New Zealand. In places like Barbados, Hawaii and Costa Rica they are tolerant of swimmers and snorkellers. Nesting beaches in Florida, Costa Rica and Puerto Rico can sometimes be visited with expert guides.

Leopard *Panthera pardus*

WHAT For many wildlife watchers on a safari, the big cat that gives the most thrills (or chills) is not the lion but the leopard. Powerful, versatile and solitary, the leopard is largely a nocturnal hunter, making them less likely to be encountered than lions and their preference for living among dense bush or rocks (all the better from which to ambush prey) doesn't help. Look up into trees, where they typically stash their prey – antelope, pigs, and occasionally livestock – out of reach of scavengers. Leopards are distributed widely across sub-Saharan Africa and also the Subcontinent and Southeast Asia. In India there are even urban leopards living in some cities. **WHERE** On the African continent, Kruger National Park in South Africa has a large population of leopards (about 1000) and is very accessible by car (Johannesburg is the closest major city). In Asia, Sri Lanka's Yala National Park on the east of the island is famed for its leopard-spotting potential.

THE A-Z OF WILDLIFE WATCHING

Leopard seal *Hydrurga leptonyx*

WHAT It can grow to 3m in length, weigh 600kg and its mouthful of serrated teeth are the match of its land-dwelling namesake. The leopard seal is a penguin's worst nightmare and quite possibly yours, should you find yourself face to face with one in the Southern Ocean. Fish, squid and at least six species of penguin – which they ambush as the birds make their way to and from the ocean – are their usual prey but larger leopard seals may also target other species of seal. In turn, their only natural enemy is the orca. **WHERE** On an Antarctic cruise, look out for leopard seals resting on ice floes. Get too close and you may be warned off with a growl. Leopard seals range widely so are unpredictable sightings. It is thought that they move northward to outlying sub-Antarctic islands during the southern winter and have been sighted around Tasmania.

© Jonathan Gregson | Lonely Planet

Lion *Panthera leo*

WHAT The image of this most celebrated of big cats might be familiar to the point of cliché. But fear not, in the wild these mammalian megastars retain every ounce of their muscle-packed majesty and mystique. **WHERE** Lions are a highlight of Kenya's Masai Mara and the Serengeti and Ngorongoro Crater National Parks in Tanzania, but spectacular sightings can also be had at the slightly lesser known parks of South Luangwa and Kafue in Zambia or the Okavango Delta or Chobe National Park in Botswana. As apex predators, by definition lions cover a large area, so choose an expert guide and time your visit carefully – the late dry season brings both predators and prey closer to rivers and watering holes. Or for a lion encounter with a difference, Indian's Gir Forest National Park is one of the last refuges of the short-maned Asiatic lion.

Little penguin (blue penguin, fairy penguin)
Eudyptula minor

WHAT The little penguin is roughly a quarter the height of its emperor cousin and one twentieth as heavy, but what it lack in stature, it makes up for in charisma. The spectacle of these sometimes noisy birds tumbling from the waves at dusk and waddling up beaches to their home burrows has become a staple of wildlife tourism in New Zealand and southern Australia.

WHERE Penguins can be seen at sea in sheltered waters around much of New Zealand, and organised watching sessions take place in several coastal sites, including Oamaru and Taiaroa Headlands near Dunedin. Following severe declines in little penguin numbers on Kangaroo Island, Tasmania has become the principle penguin-watching location in Australia, with watches taking place from September to March at locations including Penguin, Burnie and Bicheno.

Lobster *Homarus gammarus*

WHAT While condemned lobsters are easy enough to see in restaurant tanks or cages stacked on quaysides, this is a poor substitute for these crustacean big guns in the wild. In daylight hours they are mostly likely to be found lurking in a rocky crevice, but a torchlight search might reveal them stalking their seabed domain in search of smaller invertebrate prey. In life their robust exoskeletons vary from indigo to orange, green or black, but like other crustaceans they change colour when cooked, as the proteins that bind and mask the red pigment astaxanthin denature when heated. **WHERE** Seeing lobsters in their natural habitat requires a night dive or torchlight searching large rockpools close to the low tide mark. Rocky coastlines along the British Isles are a good spot for seeing the European species. A very closely related species occurs on the other sides of the Atlantic.

THE A-Z OF WILDLIFE WATCHING

Lowland streaked tenrec
Hemicentetes semispinosus

WHAT Even in a land famed for its unconventional wildlife, this punkish little Malagasy mammal is an oddity. Almost unbelievably, as a member of the group of mammals known as Afrotheria, it is more closely related to the aardvark, elephants, golden moles and manatees than to the shrew-like insectivores it resembles. The yellow-streaked fur is interspersed with spines, including barbed ones that can be ejected into the flesh of an attacker, and unbarbed ones which can be rubbed together to produce sound. This so-called 'stridulation' is usually associated with insects, and the streaked tenrec is the only mammal known to do it.

WHERE Streaked tenrecs are relatively common in forested parts of eastern Madagascar, where they occasionally even enter houses. With a little luck you may spot one in Marojejy National Park or Andasibe-Mantadia National Park.

Iberian lynx
Lynx pardinus

WHAT The Iberian lynx may be half the size of its Eurasian and North American cousins, but with its sleek spotted coat and face framed by black ear tufts and a beardy ruff, it has supermodel good looks. Fifteen years ago its conservation status was Critical, with fewer than 100 individuals surviving, of which only 25 were females. Thanks to intensive conservation the total number has increased to more than 400, and there is every chance of seeing the species in one of its two well-studied strongholds in southern Spain.

WHERE The majority of Iberian lynx are still to be found in Coto Doñana National Park and the Sierra Morena in Andalucía, southern Spain, but the species has recently spread into neighbouring Extremadura and a small reintroduced population has been established around Guadiana Natural Park in southeast Portugal.

Lyrebird *Menura novaehollandiae*

WHAT Shhh! What's that sound? Is R2D2 lost in this forest? The superb lyrebird (that's its name not an adjective) is famed for its skills of mimicry, copying the songs of other birds to create extraordinary medleys. This is one of the world's largest songbirds, but despite its vocal mastery and an extravagant mating display that utilises the male's elaborate long curlicued tail feathers, it's an extremely shy and stealthy bird, which is why it might seem rarer than it actually is. An encounter with these pheasant-sized birds is always rewarding because they lend a little flamboyance to the forest floor. **WHERE** The superb lyrebird of Victoria prefers forest and some places where they're prevalent include the Yarra Ranges National Park, northeast of Melbourne, and the Dandenongs National Park to the southeast. If you're quiet and venture from the main tracks, listen out for their songs. Mating displays happen in small clearings.

© Justin Foulkes / Lonely Planet

© Scott Portelli | Getty Images

Manatee *Trichechus manatus*

WHAT Don't be fooled by the superficially seal-like body. Manatees are more closely related to elephants than seals, and like their distant terrestrial cousins, they are confirmed herbivores. The West Indian is the largest of three species (the others being the Amazonian and African), and the easiest to see, especially in Florida, where the population is increasing thanks to conservation and tourism value. Manatees favour warm shallow coastal waters and rivers with abundant plantlife. **WHERE** You'll be spoiled for choice of manatee tours around Crystal River and Blue Springs in Florida, with opportunities to watch from boats, kayaks and boardwalks. Manatees can also be seen taking advantage of the warm water discharges of power stations at Apollo Beach and Fort Myers.

THE A-Z OF WILDLIFE WATCHING

Mandrill
Mandrillus sphinx

WHAT Mandrills like company. At least females and youngsters do: their gatherings (known as hordes) are often several hundred. They move with steady purpose through the forests of equatorial West Africa, feeding as they go and camping in a different place each night. Hordes are orderly but noisy, with shrieks, whistles and chatters, and never more so than during the breeding season (June to October) when solitary males appear to claim mates. Uniquely among mammals, dominant males sport red and blue stripes and swellings around the nose, and equally lurid colouration on the rump, with the intensity of colour relating to levels of testosterone being produced. **WHERE** Because mandrills are always on the move, seeing them in the wild often requires a lengthy trek through dense forest somewhere like Lekedi Park or Lopé National Park in Gabon, or the Dja Faunal Reserve in Cameroon. The Limbe Wildlife Centre in Cameroon offers sightings in a more enclosed setting.

Manta ray *Manta spp*

WHAT The first impression of a manta ray is probably its size ('wingspans' can exceed 6m), quickly followed by surprise that so huge an animal can move with such grace. Mutual curiosity makes an underwater encounter with these gentle giants (half-shark, half-flying carpet) an unforgettable experience – indeed mantas often appear to seek out the company of divers. **WHERE** Snorkelling and diving destinations with year-round opportunities to see manta include Kona in Hawaii, Cabo Marshall in Galapagos, the Yap archipelago in Micronesia and Coral Bay on Australia's Ningaloo Reef. If you prefer to stay out of the water, head to Mexico's Sea of Cortez in search of mobula rays. The communal leaping displays performed by these acrobatic manta cousins are best observed from a boat, and the spectacle is all the more appealing because no one knows exactly why they do it.

Mantis shrimp
Stomatopoda spp

WHAT Firstly, the mantis shrimp is not a shrimp. It's a stomatopod more closely related to lobsters. But this crustacean is definitely a killing machine. There are about 400 species of stomatopod and they employ a variety of incredible weapons. Some, such as the peacock mantis shrimp (right), have super-strong smashers (that's a technical term) that can be released at the speed of a bullet to stun victims and crack shells (or the glass of an aquarium). Others have barbed spears with which they can ambush and impale significantly larger sea life. Their eyes are equally extraordinary and allow the stomatopod to see things extremely quickly and also a greater range of colours than us. In short, if they were any larger than the 10-40cm they grow to, we'd be in trouble.

WHERE Stomatopods prefer warm shallow water in the Indian and Pacific oceans. The largest species, the zebra mantis shrimp inhabits sandy ocean floors from East Africa to Hawaii.

© Reinhard Dirscherl | Alamy Stock Photo

© Kimberly Shavender | Shutterstock

© Philip Lee Harvey | Lonely Planet

Marine iguana *Amblyrhynchus cristatus*

WHAT Times have changed since Charles Darwin referred to Galapagos marine iguanas as 'disgusting clumsy lizards' and 'imps of darkness'. Now these extraordinary marine reptiles are celebrated as unique examples of speciation. Perhaps Darwin never got to see them underwater, where they swim with eel-like grace, then lock grappling-hook claws to the rocky sea bed while snatching hasty mouthfuls of algae as sea lions swirl around them and human divers or snorkellers look on. Dives seldom last long, not only because the iguanas breathe air, but because the cold water rapidly robs them of precious body heat accumulated by sunbathing on the black volcanic rocks for which their colouring is a perfect match.

WHERE You can swim or dive with marine iguanas off the active volcanic island of Fernandina, or join guided groups to watch from boats or visit the breeding colony at Punta Espinosa.

Mata mata turtle *Chelus fimbriata*

WHAT It would be hard to make up a more fantastical-looking reptile than South America's mata mata, but once you accept that the creature before you is real, you might still be forgiven for imagining it had suffered an accident involving a large weight falling from a great height. But no, all is well. The flattened body, extendable neck and nozzle snout are all adaptations to hanging out in shallow water waiting to ambush passing prey – mainly aquatic invertebrates and small fish. The carapace of the Orinoco variety is broadly oval, while those from the Amazon are more rectangular. **WHERE** Mata matas feature among the 120 species of reptile recorded in the extraordinary biodiversity hotspot of Ecuador's Yasuní Biosphere Reserve. They're not easy to find, but while searching you might make a start ticking off the 150 frog, 600 bird and 200 mammal species also present.

Meerkat (suricate) *Suricata suricatta*

WHAT If you arrive early enough at a meerkat colony, you'll witness the morning routine of grooming and sunbathing – the latter takes place standing on two legs or sitting on the haunches to expose the sparsely haired, dark-skinned belly, which absorbs heat more efficiently than other parts of the body. The same posture is used later in the day by individuals taking turns at sentry duty, looking out for predators while the rest of the clan feed. Listen for alarm calls, which differ according to the type of predator and the urgency of the threat. **WHERE** Meerkat clans occur throughout much of the Namib and Kalahari Deserts. The long-running Kalahari Meerkat Project, studying habituated clans in South Africa's Kuruman River Reserve, regularly takes on volunteers.

THE A-Z OF WILDLIFE WATCHING

Mexican (Brazilian) free-tailed bat
Tadarida brasiliensis

WHAT For a spectacle of mammalian numbers, nothing beats the evening emergence of free-tailed bats. Colonies can be millions strong and many are migratory, travelling 1000km or more from wintering areas in Central America to summer sites able to supply the vast quantities of insects needed to sustain them.

WHERE The largest known free-tailed bat roost (also the largest known gathering of mammals anywhere in the world), can be seen at Bracken Cave, near San Antonio, Texas, where almost 20 million individuals gather between March and October. Many smaller colonies are highly accessible, such as the 1.5 million-strong summer roost under the Congress Avenue Bridge in Austin, whose members consume between four and nine tonnes of flying insects per night.

© Danita Delimont | Alamy Stock Photo

Monarch butterfly *Danaus plexippus*

WHAT Though handsome, this insect's fame is all about numbers – winter colonies in Mexico can include millions, even billions, of individuals. Monarchs are also known for epic migrations which carry them as far north as Canada to breed, but because individual butterflies do not live long enough to make a complete round trip, several generations are involved in one annual cycle, and they are guided by instinct alone. **WHERE** At the Monarch Biosphere Reserve, 100km northwest of Mexico City, a number of monarch colonies are open to visitors, with the largest at El Rosario. For a wilder, less commercial experience, try Piedra Herrada, south of Mexico City. The winter colonies in California, such as Pismo Beach and Goleta, are smaller, but still astounding. One of the largest and most accessible summer breeding sites is at Point Pelee on the northern shore of Lake Erie, Ontario.

THE A-Z OF WILDLIFE WATCHING

Moose (Eurasian elk) *Alces alces*

WHAT The world's largest deer is a hugely impressive denizen of northern forests and lakelands. Apart from mothers with calves, they are solitary, but in some areas or Scandinavia, Russia and North America it's possible to encounter several individuals a day. Moose can be aggressive if approached too closely. All four legs can kick powerfully, forwards, backwards and to the side. Watch for warning signs such as glaring, flattening of ears or raised hackles, and be ready to run. **WHERE** The state of Maine, with its abundant lakes, boasts the greatest concentration of moose in the contiguous US, and moose tours (often by boat) are easy to find. In Scandinavia, most sightings are from cars on forest roads, and at least one operator at Skinnskatteberg near Stockholm claims a 100% record of finding wild moose.

Mountain gorilla
Gorilla beringei beringei

WHAT This distinct subspecies of eastern gorilla became synonymous with the work of the late Dian Fossey and with the birth of ecotourism – an industry that has contributed significantly to the survival of the subspecies through decades of adversity including habitat destruction, hunting, disease and devastating human conflict. Compared to their lowland cousins, mountain gorillas are thicker furred, allowing them to survive at altitudes between 2400m and almost 4000m. Though wild, the remaining gorillas are habituated to human presence and benefit from veterinary attention as part of efforts to boost numbers. **WHERE** There are two populations of mountain gorilla, one in the Virunga Mountains in the border area between Rwanda, Uganda and the Democratic of Congo, and the other in Bwindi Impenetrable National Park, Uganda. Both populations are growing thanks to intensive conservation but remain Critically Endangered.

Mountain lion (puma, cougar, catamount, Florida panther)
Puma concolor

WHAT Scientifically speaking, this is a small cat, differing from the pantherine big cats in its ability to purr, but not roar. But make no mistake, a puma is a huge, powerful predator and definitely one to watch from a distance. Despite the alternative name 'mountain lion', pumas are not restricted to high ground, and in many cases often live close to human communities, even on the outskirts of large cities.

WHERE Pumas occupy a vast species range from Candian Yukon to the southern Andes. The highest density (and the highest frequency of attacks on humans) is on Vancouver Island, but even here, sightings are rare. Perhaps the best opportunities to watch pumas safely are in Patagonia, where several operators run guided puma tours. The tiny population in Florida (where they are known as panthers) can be glimpsed in Everglades National Park and adjoining protected areas.

© Vince Burton | Alamy Stock Photo

© Justin Foulkes | Lonely Planet

© imageBROKER | Alamy Stock Photo

Mouse lemur *Microcebus spp*

WHAT Genetic research in recent years has revised the number of known species of mouse lemur from two to more than 20 – many of them highly endangered. Most are nocturnal tree-dwelling omnivores and live in female-dominated family groups. They include the world's smallest primate, Madame Berthe's mouse lemur (*M berthae*), which weighs as little as 30g. The various species look very similar – it's likely the animals themselves rely on non-visual cues such as calls to recognise potential mates. Regardless of species, an encounter with any of these enchanting wide-eyed miniatures is a privilege. **WHERE** Mouse lemurs can be seen in many areas of dry forest in western Madagascar. Kirindy Forest Reserve is home to several species, including Madam Berthe's. Avoid the dry season (April to October), when females are almost completely inactive.

THE A-Z OF WILDLIFE WATCHING

Musk ox
Ovibos moschatus

WHAT The musk ox is an immense Arctic goat, up to 2.5m long and endowed with large drooping horns, the bases of which shield the head in a massive thickness of bone – an effective deterrent against its few predators, especially when used in defensive formations around vulnerable members of the herd. Thick coats and an ability to graze or browse almost any vegetation serve these ultra-hardy mammals well in exposed tundra landscapes.

WHERE The natural strongholds of the musk ox lie in the remote Arctic outposts of the Canadian Northwest Territories and Greenland. Around half the world population lives on Banks Island, where a visit to Aulavik National Park generally requires the chartering of a plane and wilderness camping. The vast expanse of Northeast Greenland National Park (the world's largest) is a similarly ambitious destination. More accessible introduced and reintroduced herds can be seen in Québec (Nunavik) and Alaska (Seward Peninsula).

Naked mole rat
Heterocephalus glaber

WHAT A species that seems to defy zoological convention in almost every aspect of its extraordinary life, the naked mole rat is blind and virtually hairless, its body temperature varies wildly according to ambient conditions, and it can survive oxygen depletion that would be lethal to other mammals. Like worker bees, most individuals surrender their right to reproduce to support the breeding of a single queen. Most spend their entire lifetime below ground, so seeing one of these bizarre little rodents in the wild takes a bit of serendipity. Most sightings are at night as dispersing individuals set out to establish new colonies. These atypical pioneers appear to prepare for their endeavour by working less and accumulating large reserves of fat.

WHERE Meru National Park, Kenya is home to good populations of naked mole rats and the site of a long-running study of their unique biology and ecology.

Namib fog-basking beetle *Stenocara gracilipes*

WHAT It looks like insect yoga, but the early morning posturing of this specialist beetle is a matter of survival in one of the driest regions of the planet. Life here is possible only for the few species able to convert the moisture in dense sea fogs into a usable form. The fog beetle makes an arduous daily pilgrimage to the crest of a sand dune and elevates its rear end on long spindly legs until it appears to be standing on its head. Beads of water condense on the wingcases, adhering by microscopic forces of attraction until they reach a critical mass, when gravity rolls them down to the beetle's mouth. **WHERE** The fog beetle is one of the smaller wonders of the Namib Desert. It can be found at the NamibRand Nature Reserve and throughout Skeleton Coast National Park.

Narwhal *Monodon monoceros*

WHAT As the Arctic summer gathers pace, ice fractures and drifts, opening routes into the productive polar seas. This frontier is the place to find unicorns – or the closest thing to them that nature can deliver. Narwhals are cousins of beluga whales, with which they occasionally associate. Often the first sign that a pod is in the area is the sight of a spiralling 'horn' piercing the water like King Arthur's sword Excalibur. This extraordinary structure is a canine tooth, which pierces the upper lip in young males and continues to grow throughout life, occasionally exceeding 2.5m in length. Roughly one in 500 males grows two tusks.
WHERE Narwhals frequent the edges of the Arctic ice and can be watched from bases in the Nunavut communities of Pond Inlet, Resolute and Arctic Bay.

THE A-Z OF WILDLIFE WATCHING

Nēnē (Hawaiian goose) *Branta sandvicensis*

WHAT By 1952, only 30 of Hawaii's endemic goose survived on the archipelago thanks to hunting and predation by introduced rats, mongooses and pigs. The fortunes of these docile birds have improved since then, but they remain the world's rarest goose. **WHERE** For several years, the best place to see the state bird of Hawaii was 11,000km away in rural England, at the Slimbridge Wetland Cenre in Gloucestershire. Captive breeding here during the 1950s provided an insurance policy and was instrumental in saving the species from extinction. Many tame nēnēs still live here and at other WWT reserves, trailing visitors in the hope of hand-outs of food. The population in Hawaii now numbers around 800, with wild birds at Haleakala National Park on Maui and Hawaii Volcanoes National Park on Big Island.

Nightingale
Luscinia megarhynchos

WHAT Among the most celebrated of all small birds, the nightingale could scarcely be more mundane to look at. Its song, however, is anything but drab. The outpourings of unattached males, usually delivered from thickets of vegetation as night falls in early summer, are sounds of unrivalled complexity and clarity – rivers of song, with a magic and poetry all their own. **WHERE** The nightingale has a special place in human culture throughout its range, which covers much of Europe and southern Asia. A reliable place to hear the species in Britain is the rewilded landscape around Knepp Castle in Sussex.

Northern gannet *Morus bassanus*

WHAT From a sky of gleaming wings, bodies fold suddenly into living darts and plummet into the sea at speeds of up to 100kph. Northern gannets use this breathtaking technique to capture small fish, which are swallowed before the bird leaves the water. **WHERE** The British Isles are the centre of distribution for this spectacular seabird and home to almost 70% of the world population. There are large colonies at Bempton Cliffs in North Yorkshire, the Welsh island of Skokholm, and in the Shetland Isles. But there's nowhere more impressive to see the species than the dramatic natural fortress for which it is scientifically named – Bass Rock, in the Moray Firth. The 75,000 nesting pairs that arrive here in summer occupy almost every inch of rock. Boat trips depart daily, or in calm conditions the more adventurous might consider a tour by kayak.

Numbat
Myrmecobius fasciatus

WHAT In the high-contrast light and shade of Western Australia's dry forests, with luck and patience on your side, you may see a patch of sun-streaked bark start to move on dainty trotting paws. Marsupials don't come any prettier than the diminutive numbat, an enchanting cousin of the extinct thylacine and a voracious eater, feeding exclusively on up to 20,000 ants and termites in a day.

WHERE Native numbats survive in the jarrah and wandoo woodlands of Dryandra and Tone State Forest in Western Australia, and at nine further sanctuary areas where captive bred animals have been reintroduced and non-native predators (mainly foxes) are controlled or fenced out. These sites include Boyagin Nature Reserve and Batalling Forest (WA), Yookamurra Sanctuary in South Australia and Scotia Sanctuary in New South Wales.

Ocelot
Leopardus pardalis

WHAT In the dappled light of its forest home, the boldly patterned coat of this stealthy hunter – somewhere between spotty and stripey – becomes a cloak of near-invisibility. The ocelot is a small but powerful cat, no threat to humans, but deadly to a wide range of small- to medium-size prey including rabbits, opossums, armadillos, monkeys and lizards.

WHERE Ocelots can be glimpsed unpredictably in many parts of their huge range, but more reliable opportunities to see and photograph them are also offered in the Brazilian Pantanal, and Costa Rica's Monteverde Cloud Forest Reserve or Corcovado or Santa Rosa National Parks. A small population of about 35 animals survives at the Laguna Atascosa National Wildlife Refuge in Texas.

Okapi
Okapia johnstoni

WHAT Perhaps more than any other animal, the okapi embodies the heart of Africa. Where else but in this vast, scarcely accessible rainforest could such a large and extraordinary-looking mammal live unknown to western science until the early 20th century? The okapi is solitary, timid and deeply secretive so an encounter is truly something to treasure. Live in the moment – there may not be time for photographs before that unmistakeable stripy backside retreats into the forest and disappears.

WHERE The only place to see wild okapi is in the Democratic Republic of Congo. Sadly, continuing attacks on staff and facilities at the world heritage-listed Okapi Wildlife Reserve have put the site off-limits to tourists, but there's a chance of sightings in Maiko National Park and in the Semliki Valley of Virunga National Park, where a search might be combined with a visit to the mountain gorillas.

Olm
Proteus anguinus

WHAT In days of yore, when heavy rain fell on the limestone landscape of the western Balkans, the huge amounts of water disgorged from myriad cave systems sometimes washed baby dragons from their nests and into the world above. At least that was how 17th-century legend explained the appearance of blind creatures with pink, snakelike bodies and spindly limbs. In fact the olm is a large cave-dwelling amphibian.

WHERE Olms are endemic to the southwestern Balkans. The species is particularly celebrated in Slovenia, and nowhere more so than in Postojna, a global centre for speleobiology, the branch of science dealing with cave life. Several specimens can be seen on showcave tours, and in 2016 the first eggs laid by a captive female hatched successfully in a blaze of publicity.

© Blickwinkel | Alamy Stock Photo

© Mbbirdy | Getty Images

Orangutan
Pongo pygmaeus and *Pongo abelii*

WHAT In many ways orangutans are poster species for anthropogenic extinction. With their habitat shrinking at a catastrophic rate, the best chances of seeing them are often around refuge areas where rehabilitated or relocated individuals (often rescued from the last tree standing in their original homes) have been released. You're likely to come away with bittersweet memories and a renewed determination to avoid the use of palm oil – the chief economic driver of habitat destruction.

WHERE To see Bornean orangutans (*Pongo pygmaeus*), visit Tanjung Puting National Park in Kalimantan or the Danum Valley Field Centre and Tabin Wildlife Reserve, both in Sabah. On Sumatra, wild and rehabilitated Sumatran orangutans (*Pongo abelii*) still gather around the former refuge in Gunung Leuser National Park. Try to support the conservation efforts – income from responsible orangtuan tourism may be instrumental in saving both species.

© Matt Munro | Lonely Planet

Orca
Orcinus orca

WHAT Orca, or killer whales, have not been christened lightly. They're arguably the ocean's most complete predator and pods are capable of separating young whales from their mothers, in addition to hunting seals and even killing great white sharks. What makes orca so formidable? It's not just their size, although at up to 9m in length and six tons in weight, they're the largest of the dolphin family. Rather it's their intelligence. Different populations of orca around the world have devised techniques for hunting their favoured prey, whether that's washing seals off ice floes in the Antarctic, chasing sea lions onto beaches in Patagonia, herding herring together in Norwegian fjords or taking down grey whales along the Mexican and Californian coast. **WHERE** Three places with frequent orca sightings are around Vancouver Island in British Columbia, in the fjords of northern Norway, and around the Bay of Islands in northern New Zealand.

© RobynPhoto | Getty Images

Ostrich *Struthio camelus*

WHAT Flightlessness is an odd strategy for a bird living alongside a wide range of large predators, and the ostrich only gets away with it by virtue of its size and speed – it is both the largest and fastest-running bird. Its short wings, not used for flight for 56 million years, now serve various functions, including stabilisation, temperature control, steering and display, and between April and September pairs may be seen fanning and posturing as a prelude to mating. The blue-necked ostriches or Somali ostriches of the Horn of Africa were recently recognised as a separate species, *Struthio molybdophanes*. **WHERE** Wild ostriches can be seen in many dry areas of Africa, from the Sahel to South Africa. They are increasingly widely farmed around the world and many farms open their doors to the public – but attitudes to welfare vary, with some offering visitors the dubious privilege of riding or sitting on a bird's back.

Pacific octopus *Enteroctopus dofleini*

WHAT The largest known octopus species (occasionally 8m across) is also one of the smartest animals on the planet, with skills worthy of a Marvel superhero. It is able to change the form, colour and texture of its body for camouflage or communication. It is muscular and powerful, yet soft and flexible enough to squeeze through absurdly small gaps. Its tentacles can grasp and manipulate with extraordinary dexterity and the entire body surface is highly sensitive to touch and taste. Your curiosity during an encounter is likely to be mutual.

WHERE It's possible to join guided octopus dives in several part of the species' range around the north Pacific Rim. Sightings are reliable in the Seattle area, especially in spring when females are tending eggs, but bear in mind this is their one chance to breed, as they die soon after their young hatch.

Pangolin
Smutsia temminckii

WHAT It looks like a giant pine cone that has fallen and rolled far beyond its parent tree...until it unrolls, sprouts legs and a long tapering tail, and ambles off, snuffling noisily in its relentless search for ant and termite nests. Of all the diverse body coverings vertebrate animals have developed from the versatile hair-, scale-, horn- and feather-forming protein keratin, the scales of the pangolin (a mammal, not a reptile) are the most incongruous. Like rhinoceroses, Cape pangolins pay a heavy price for human obsession with their keratinaceous outgrowths – they are the world's most poached and trafficked mammals and thus among the most severely threatened.

WHERE Namibia is a centre for Cape pangolin research; tour groups can sometimes contribute to tracking studies carried out at the private reserves such as Mundulea and Erindi.

Panther chameleon *Furcifer pardalis*

WHAT Independently swivelling gun-turret eyes and an uncanny ability to change colour have earned the chameleons a special place in Malagasy folklore. Males are larger and typically more colourful than females – in fact this species is arguably the most luridly technicolour of all. Contrary to popular myth, the ability to vary skin pigmentation is not an attempt to blend in with surroundings, but a means of signalling mood and intent to other chameleons. **WHERE** Chameleons are a speciality of several Malagasy reserve areas, among them the Analamozaotra Special Reserve within Andasibe-Mantadia National Park and Lokobe Reserve on the island of Nosy Be. The range of colours varies regionally, so while the population on Nosy Be shows a preference for blue, those from Andasibe-Mantadia are more likely to flaunt shades of red. Introduced populations also exist on Réunion and Mauritius.

Peacock spider
Maratus spp

WHAT In the dry scrublands of Australia, an audition of sorts has begun. The judge is female and the performer is a hopeful suitor. He salutes her with two black and white legs, performs a series of rapid semaphore-like signals, and builds to a piece de resistance – the raising of a multicoloured metallic disc on his abdomen. The energy, colour and ostentation of the display is worthy of a bird of paradise, but this dancing work of art is only a few millimetres long, and not a bird, but a variety of jumping spider. If the female isn't impressed (and sometimes even if she is), she'll eat him.

WHERE Peacock spiders are widespread in dry scrublands and open woodlands across Australia (including Tasmania), with new species almost certainly awaiting discovery. Spotting them requires patience, attention to detail, and a willingness to spend time observing quietly.

Great white pelican *Pelecanus onocrotalus*

WHAT With its deep body, colossal bucket-bill and a wingspan often exceeding 3m, this is one of the largest pelican species. It is also highly gregarious, and the sight and sound of a flock several hundred strong making a barely controlled aquatic crash-landing is akin to experiencing the sky falling in.

WHERE White pelicans thrive in the many shallow lakes of the Great Rift Valley. The huge expanse of Lake Rukwa in Tanzania, very much off the beaten tourist track, is home to Africa's largest breeding population, with the next most significant centred on Lake Shala in Ethiopia's Abidjatta-Shalla National Park. The flocks at Lake Nakuru National Park in Kenya are smaller but still impressive, and have the benefit of accessibility, being just two hours away from Nairobi.

Peregrine falcon *Falco peregrinus*

WHAT 'He had another thousand feet to fall but now he fell sheer, shimmering down through dazzling sunlight, heart-shaped, like a heart in flames.' So JA Baker describes a peregrine falcon's dive towards an unwitting partridge in his seminal book *The Peregrine*. This is the fastest animal on earth: a medium-sized, monochrome falcon that folds in its wings and stoops at 320kph before hitting its target. Several varieties are widespread around the world but you may be surprised where you can see one. **WHERE** Cities. Yes, peregrines have adapted to the urban environment better than many birds of prey. Cities such as New York and London offer high vantage points and an abundance of food in the form of pigeons. Peregrine pairs have nested on top of Tate Modern's chimney in London and use the Empire State Building as a hunter's lookout. Bird-watching tours of both cities may feature peregrines.

Pine marten
Martes martes

WHAT An exceptionally lithe tree dweller found across much of Europe, the pine marten has undergone an encouraging recovering in Britain, where it was previously persecuted to the brink of extinction. Naturally nocturnal and secretive, pine martens can become bold where they are habituated to people. Their natural diet includes a variety of small mammals, birds and eggs, but they also eat fruit and are said to be incapable of resisting jam sandwiches. **WHERE** The British stronghold for pine martens is the Highlands of Scotland, where well established hides at venues including Aigas Field Center (Inverness-shire), Speyside Wildlife Centre near Aviemore and Kindrogan Field Centre in Perthshire offer excellent viewings. Guesthouses and cafes often advertise grounds with pine martens. A reintroduced population is becoming established in mid-Wales and recent records in northern England fuel hopes of a further recovery there.

Pink fairy armadillo *Chlamyphorus truncates*

WHAT You'd be forgiven for thinking that this furry fondant fancy of an animal was a taxidermic fake, manufactured for whimsy or to dupe an unwary collector during the great age of global exploration. But the pink fairy armadillo is most definitely real, if difficult to spot. The reduced eyes, huge blunt claws and mole-like body are clues to its burrowing lifestyle. The species is specialised to the degree that it has proved virtually impossible to keep in captivity, and it also appears highly susceptible to stress in the wild, where it is likely to be threatened by a variety of agricultural practices. A chance encounter is thus a true moment to treasure. **WHERE** Central Argentina, with the best chances of sightings at night after heavy rain in protected areas such as the Lihué Calel National Park.

THE A-Z OF WILDLIFE WATCHING

Pink river dolphin (Amazon river dolphin, bufeo, boto) *Inia geoffrensis*

WHAT A long, narrow snout, piggy eyes, slightly saggy skin and a salmon pink belly...there's a lot about this freshwater cetacean that seems undolphinlike. Its flexible spine allows it to weave through the submerged trunks of a flooded forest, navigating and finding food by echolocation, its tiny eyes all but useless in the tea-coloured water. But it shares the curiosity and acrobatic tendencies of its marine relatives, often following boats and occasionally breaching, to the delight of onlookers. **WHERE** Botos are widely distributed in the side channels and lakes of the Amazon and Orinoco Rivers, especially around confluences. Promising destinations include Peru's vast Pacaya Samiria National Park and the less developed Parque Nacional Amacayacu in Colombia. The Bolivian subspecies, somewhat less pink than elsewhere, can be seen on the Yacuma and Marmoré Rivers, among others.

Plainfin midshipman (or toadfish) *Porichthys notatus*

WHAT For most of the year these are deepwater fish, remarkable for their rows of blue light-emitting photophores, which lure prey and possibly camouflage the fish against the bright water surface. Come spring, however, males move to the shallows, find a secure rocky lair, and then, amazingly, they begin to hum, loud enough to disturb people sleeping in boats or beach houses. The drone is a serenade to potential mates, generated by vibrations of the swimbladder, an air sac normally used to regulate buoyancy. Successful males will remain at their post for several weeks, protecting the fertilised eggs as they develop. **WHERE** Pacific coasts of North America, from southern Alaska to Baja California. At Elkhorn Slough in California, fish may be exposed to the air for a few hours at low tide and can be discovered by carefully turning rocks close to the water.

THE A-Z OF WILDLIFE WATCHING

© Danita Delimont | Alamy Stock Photo

© Justinreznick | Getty Images

Polar bear *Ursus maritimus*

WHAT Ironically, the bear most qualified to make you feel small knows that feeling well, spending much of its life alone in one of the emptiest habitats on Earth – the Arctic sea ice. Polar bears might just as well be named sea bears, being equally comfortable on land, ice, or in water. The spectacular coat that sets them apart from other bears is not only an adaptation to extreme cold, but also serves as a buoyancy aid – each colourless hair contains a central air space. The best opportunities for seeing polar bears are in summer, when ice-melt forces them onto land, where they switch from hunting seals to a mixed diet including berries and carrion. **WHERE** Polar bears occupy the northern margins of Canada, Alaska, Russia, Greenland and Scandinavia. Commercial tour operators focus on Spitzbergen and the Canadian settlement of Churchill on Hudson Bay, where bears arrive in summer in unparalleled numbers.

© Peter Blackwell | www.naturepl.com

Porcupine *Hystrix cristata*

WHAT As a general rule, crested porcupines do not want to be watched, and make their displeasure clear, turning their back and erecting an impressive array of quills. Even longer than the quills are the stiff hairs that serve as sensors – any predator approaching too close will trigger a well-aimed reverse rush that will leave barbed points embedded in its face.
WHERE Crested porcupines occur in more than 30 African countries north and south of the Sahara, but their nocturnal habits and aversion to people make them difficult to spot. Your best chance of seeing one in the wild may not be in Africa at all, but in Italy, where the species' status is uncertain. Fossil remains suggest it was once native, but the current population is thought to be descended from animals introduced by the Romans. Tuscany is the centre of distribution, with regular sightings in Maremma Regional Park near Grosseto.

THE A-Z OF WILDLIFE WATCHING

Portuguese man o' war *Physalia physalis*

WHAT This infamous stinger is not one animal, but a predatory colony of conjoined individual polyps attached to a single float. Different polyps have specialist roles – some are reproductive, some are concerned purely with digesting prey and others are armed with tentacles used in hunting and defence. The stings are severe and can be delivered by detached tentacles and dead colonies, making this very much a species to admire from a distance. Look, but don't touch. **WHERE** Warm areas of the Atlantic Ocean and adjoining seas, with large drifts occasionally washing ashore. These can be difficult to predict, but where one colony is spotted, more often appear, having been carried by the same winds and currents. In the Pacific and Indian Oceans look out for the similar *Physalia utriculus* or bluebottle, a little smaller than the man o' war and with more intense blue colouration.

Praying mantis
Mantis religiosa

WHAT Stalking among foliage, this extraordinary alien-eyed bug is easily mistaken for part of the plant it inhabits. For a wide range of other small animals, this would be a fatal error. But the mantis's huge raptorial forelegs, habitually folded in a posture suggesting prayer, are poised in constant readiness to strike, and powerful enough to subdue victims as large as hummingbirds. Be warned, while mantises are not venomous, the bite of a large individual (they grow up to 9cm) can pierce human skin. **WHERE** This is the most widespread mantis species, known through much of southern Europe, Asia, North Africa and North America, where it was introduced.

Proboscis monkey *Nasalis larvatus*

WHAT This pot-bellied, web-footed, semi-aquatic monkey has no shortage of unusual features, but it is the pendulous nose of the males that earns the species its common name. Proboscis monkeys are endemic to the island of Borneo, where local nicknames refer to a perceived resemblance with early Dutch settlers. The species is best sought by boat. Listen for the honking calls of males (the larger the nose, the louder the honk) to help locate a group. **WHERE** Proboscis monkeys inhabit mangroves and waterside forests in Borneo. Close encounters can be had at a sanctuary at Labuk Bay in Sandakan in Sabah, created to save the local monkeys from habitat loss to palm oil development, and at a former zoo near Pangkalan Bun in central Kalimantan, now owned and managed by Orangutan Foundation International.

Pronghorn
Antilocapra americana

WHAT Crowned with a pair of forked, blade-like horns unlike those of any other hoofed mammal, the pronghorn is something of an oddity. Sometimes referred to as the American antelope, this handsome mammal is in fact the sole surviving member of its family and more closely related to giraffes and the okapi. It is also one of the world's supreme animal athletes, capable of short bursts of more than 80kph second only to the cheetah.

WHERE The America Prairie Reserve is an expanding patchwork of linked protected areas in central Montana. A joint project between federal, state and non-governmental organisations, it aims to connect the landscape within which pronghorns live and migrate into Alberta and Saskatchewan. Visit in autumn to see herds gathering to begin their journey north.

Przewalski's horse *Equus ferus przewalskii*

WHAT The world's only fully wild horse (not descended from domestic ancestors) is stocky and square-faced with an erect zebra-like quiff. Its ochre hide is a close match for its native steppe habitat, and it is swift enough to outrun a wolf. But speed and camouflage are no defence against rifle fire, and by 1969 the species became extinct in the wild and remained so until 1992, when a reintroduction of zoo-bred animals began.

WHERE To see this hardy ungulate in its native Mongolia, visit Khustain Nuruu (Hustai) National Park, 100km from Ulaanbaatar. This is the site of the first reintroduction of captive bred animals, and is now home to several hundred animals. Further reintroduced populations exist in the Gobi desert reserve of Takhin Tal, and beyond Mongolia in Kazakhstan, Russia, Hungary, China and in the naturally rewilding landscape around the Chernobyl Exclusion Zone in the Ukraine.

© Juniors Bildarchiv GmbH | Alamy Stock Photo

Ptarmigan
Lagopus muta

WHAT The alternative name rock ptarmigan describes this hardy grouse in summer plumage, when its grey mottling is a perfect match for lichen-covered rocks. In winter it moults to snowy white, and toughs it out in some of the harshest conditions on earth, surviving by digging in snow for frozen vegetation.

WHERE Ptarmigan occur on arctic and subarctic landscapes around almost the entire northern hemisphere. They can be viewed conveniently on the ice- and wind-scoured summit of Cairngorm in the Scottish Highlands, an ice age refuge providing a taste of the Arctic just a short cablecar ride from the relative comfort of the small town of Aviemore. A visit in winter will leave you in no doubt of the resilience of these sturdy birds, and if you're not feeling so resilient yourself, you can defrost with a hot chocolate at the suitably named Ptarmigan summit restaurant.

Python (Burmese) *Python bivittatus*

WHAT Like its close relative the Indian rock python, this handsome snake favours forests and swamps, where its giraffe-like patterning serves as excellent camouflage. The species' good looks and relatively docile nature have made it a popular pet, but there's a problem. Pythons grow fast, and while growth slows down after a couple of years, it never stops. Hence, sooner or later, pets outgrow most owners, who decide belatedly that they belong in the wild after all. **WHERE** In Florida, Burmese pythons are highly problematic aliens. Unwanted or escaped pets have devastated native wildlife, including opossums, raccoons, deer and even bobcats. In an attempt to curb their spread, local authorities periodically hold a Python Challenge in which all-comers can receive brief training and participate in a hunt. Be warned though – this is a serious control effort and captured pythons will be killed.

© Ondřej Prošický | Shutterstock

Resplendent quetzal *Pharomachrus mocinno*

WHAT It's easy to see why this large member of the trogon family was revered by both Mayan and Aztec civilisations, in which it was associated with the feathered snake god Quetzalcoatl. The iridescent emerald tail feathers were collected for ritual decoration, but in an early example of conservation the lives of the birds were spared after plucking. The plumage manages to be simultaneously decorative and cryptic in dense forest. Both male and female incubate the eggs – a feat that requires them to sit with the tail trailing out of the nest hole, where it resembles a sprouting fern. **WHERE** The resplendent quetzal is restricted to the cloud forests of Central America from southern Mexico to Panama, but is most iconic in Guatemala, where it is the national bird. The Biotopo Mario Dary Rivera nature reserve in Baja Verapaz is known locally as the Quetzal Biotope.

Quokka
Setonix brachyurus

WHAT This charismatic miniature kangaroo is one of those species that will come to find you, once you are in the right place. Quokkas evolved in Western Australia without hunting pressure from humans or introduced predators and have little innate fear of either – a factor in their drastic decline on the mainland. **WHERE** For natural history enthusiasts, a visit to Perth, Australia would not be complete without an excursion to Rottnest Island, a short ferry ride from the port of Fremantle. Here you stand a good chance of being accosted by a quokka before you've been on the island five minutes. Don't neglect your picnic bag – there are fines for feeding them, and they'll help themselves with nimble paws given a chance. Further small colonies exist on Bald Island and in a mainland reserve area at Two Peoples Bay, both near Albany.

© Catherine Sutherland | Lonely Planet

Quoll *Dasyurus viverrinus*

WHAT Small, spotted and voracious, the eastern quoll is not as cute as its cat-like appearance suggests.

It's one of Australia's few carnivorous marsupials, hunting smaller mammals, frogs, insects and young birds with a seemingly insatiable hunger.

Although regarded as 'the farmer's friend' due to their appetite for vermin, they're considered extinct from mainland Australia due to predation and extermination. It's survival of the fittest from the very start of life for a quoll: females give birth to about thirty young but have only six teats. **WHERE** Until recently, the eastern quoll was found only in Tasmania, where it is relatively widespread. The Tasmanian Devil Conservation Park near Port Arthur has some quolls if you don't spot them in the wild. But some of Tassie's quolls are being reintroduced to New South Wales in Booderee National Park near Jervis Bay.

It's hoped that the quoll will once again thrive on Australia's mainland.

Raven *Corvus corax*

WHAT Impressive size, striking jet-black plumage and native problem-solving intelligence earn these magnificent crows a powerful identity in cultures throughout their huge northern hemisphere range. They are rewarding birds to watch – youngsters are gregarious and noisy, pairs mate for life and are highly vocal and demonstrative, and courtship displays involve breathtaking aerial acrobatics. **WHERE** It's possible to experience ravens on their own terms in wild landscapes from Yellowstone to the Mongolian steppe to the English Lake District. For a guaranteed encounter with a historic and cultural angle, there's always the Tower of London, where it is said if the resident ravens leave, the monarchy and Britain will fall. Unsurprisingly, they are wing-clipped to keep them from straying far.

Red deer
Cervus elaphus

WHAT Red deer are found across Europe, but nowhere do they make a more evocative sight than in Scotland, where they are celebrated as 'monarchs of the glen' and support a buoyant stalking industry. In fact the herds here do a little too well. In the absence of their chief natural predator, the wolf, they have to be actively managed to reduce their impact on forests.

WHERE Red herds are at their most spectacular during the autumn rut, when stags reach peak condition and compete for females in contests of bellowing, strutting and sparring with their branched antlers, which are cast and regrow a little larger every year. Stag-watching can be dangerous, so it's best to take a guided tour such as those operating from Glenlivet in the Cairngorms National Park or on the Isle of Rum in the Inner Hebrides, where the red deer have been studied for several decades.

© Craig Easton | Lonely Planet

Red kangaroo *Macropus rufus*

WHAT One million years ago, Australia's ancient outback was home to *Procoptodon goliah*, a giant kangaroo standing 2m tall. Today, the title of the world's largest marsupial is held by the red kangaroo, which can stand as tall as an adult male human. Mobs of these mammals live in the searing heat of Australia's heart (unlike the smaller grey kangaroo, which is a common sight around the country's coastal settlements). Red kangaroos can cover more than 7m in one bound, travelling at 55kph. Females may carry their young joeys in their pouch for the first eight months of their life. Males are bigger, bulkier and will box rivals for mating rights. **WHERE** You'll need to get into the outback to see red 'roos: New South Wales' most remote and arid national park, Sturt, lies north of Broken Hill and has a huge population of them. Avoid visiting in summer unless you enjoy extreme heat.

Red kite *Milvus milvus*

WHAT Whether you're watching a single cruising bird or a company of hundreds around a large roost or well-known feeding area, the spectacle of red kites in flight is akin to an aerial ballet. With the aid of binoculars you'll be able to see the feather-by-feather adjustments that allow these superlative fliers to slide around the sky with effortless grace and precision.

WHERE In 1992 these harmless scavengers were on the brink of extinction in Britain following centuries of persecution. A tiny population survived in mid-Wales, sustained largely by the sympathetic attitude of one farmer. Intensive conservation and reintroduction have since reversed the fortunes of the species nationwide, but Gigrin Farm remains the place to see them up close – anything up to 400 kites show up each afternoon for a buffet of offcuts from the local abattoir.

THE A-Z OF WILDLIFE WATCHING

Red panda *Ailurus fulgens*

WHAT For years, red pandas have puzzled scientists seeking to classify them. How can they be related to their giant black-and-white namesakes when they resemble raccoons more closely in appearance and size? For now they've been given their own family, next to skunks and raccoons. They do share a largely herbivorous diet of bamboo shoots and leaves with the giant panda but are also able to eat fruits, seeds and even eggs. Fewer than 10,000 remain, largely in unpopulated parts of the Eastern Himalaya in Bhutan, Nepal, India and China. They nest in and forage among highland trees so deforestation and habitat loss is a serious problem. **WHERE** In India, they're present only in Sikkim. Singalila National Park, a short drive from Darjeeling has a population of red pandas; guides are mandatory in this park. In Nepal there is a small population in Langtang National Park, north of Kathmandu – again, a guide is recommended to track down these elusive animals.

Red squirrel *Sciurus vulgaris*

WHAT The species immortalised by Beatrix Potter as irrepressible delinquent Nutkin is these days more often painted as a victim, following its extinction from most of its English and Welsh range. The loss is attributable to the spread of introduced American grey squirrels and in particular to the virus known as squirrel pox – fatal to reds but carried by grey with no ill effects. Introduced greys are also spreading from northern Italy across the Alps. **WHERE** The native squirrels of Germany's Black Forest are as yet untroubled by introduced greys, and easy to see, especially in areas where they are regularly fed. The popular waterfall walk at Triberg is an exceptionally reliable place for sightings. In the UK, the Lake District and Kielder Forest in Northumberland boast good populations on the frontline of the battle to hold back the grey tide.

THE A-Z OF WILDLIFE WATCHING

Red wolf *Canis rufus*

WHAT The origins of this small wolf are the subject of scientific debate, with some evidence to suggest they are the result of hybridisation between grey wolves and coyotes. While the distinction is academic, full species status is important in guaranteeing continued conservation of the tiny surviving population. Of just 300 animals remaining, fewer than 50 live wild, with a further 200 in zoos and wildlife parks around the US. Fortunately, the wolves themselves have no inkling of their precarious status. **WHERE** Red wolves currently live wild in three National Wildlife Refuges within the species' restoration area on the Albemarle peninsula in northeastern North Carolina: Pocosin Lakes, Mattamuskeet and Alligator River. Sightings are far from guaranteed, but the next best thing is to hear them, and on summer evenings it's sometimes possible to experience a nerve-tingling response during guided 'Howling Safari' sessions run by staff at the Alligator River refuge.

Red-bellied piranha
Pygocentrus nattereri

WHAT Forget the movies. Frenzied attacks in which humans or other large animals are reduced to skeletons in minutes by marauding schools of mindlessly voracious piranhas are, by and large, fiction. Certainly there's a frisson to entering water inhabited by a creature with teeth sharp enough to slice flesh cleanly from bone, but unless you're bleeding, thrashing, already dead or taking a dip in a pool where starving shoals have been trapped for a very long time, these rather timid little scavengers will be far more interested in nibbling insects, plants and organic debris than taking a chunk out of you. **WHERE** Red-bellies are abundant in much of their wide range, which includes the Amazon and neighbouring river basins from northern South America to the Pantanal. Avoid the water during the dry season and at night, and always heed local advice – piranhas may be the least of your worries.

© Rolf Nussbaumer Photography | Alamy Stock Photo

Red-billed streamertail (doctor bird) *Trochilus polytmus*

WHAT In the opening lines to his Bond novel For Your Eyes Only, Ian Fleming described this dazzling hummingbird as the most beautiful bird in Jamaica, possibly the world. It's certainly up there with the best, and, delightfully, not difficult to find on the island. Only the males sport the streamers for which the species is named – they are elongated tail feathers, one and a half times as long as the rest of the body. Its unusual scalloped structure creates a strange, high-pitched whirring sound as the bird flies. **WHERE** Streamertails are the most numerous hummingbirds on Jamaica, and can be seen across much of the island, including the Blue and John Crow Mountains National Park. For a magical close-up encounter, visit Rocklands Bird Sanctuary in Montego Bay, where wild streamertails will hum in to perch on your finger while they sip from a hand-held feeder.

Red-crowned crane *Grus japonensis*

WHAT If scores were to be awarded to birds for best mating dances, the endangered red-crowned crane of East Asia would be in the top ten and possibly in the dance-off for a podium place. Their costume – an elegant ensemble of white plumage with black trim, long legs and red flash on their head – earns high marks. But it's their dancing that mesmerises. Crane couples mate for life and reaffirm their bonds with synchronised displays of jumping, bowing, spinning and fancy footwork. But these birds, which stand 1.5m tall, also dance when alone and just wanting to express themselves. **WHERE** Red-crowned cranes are found in China and South Korea but are most usually associated with Japan where populations reside on the northern island of Hokkaido. Sightings (best in winter) are guaranteed at the Tsurui-Ito Tancho Sanctuary on the east side of Hokkaido. The sanctuary is reached from Kushiro airport.

© David Tipling | Getty Images

Red-eyed tree frog *Agalychnis callidryas*

WHAT This gaudy amphibian might have been designed by an ad agency as poster-species for Central America's rainforests, but its eye-catching appearance serves a far more life-and-death function than that; the combination of red, green, orange and blue is strident enough to dazzle potential predators. The effect might be momentary as the hunter adjusts to what it is seeing, but that moment is enough to enhance the frog's chances of escape. **WHERE** Costa Rica is undisputedly the frog capital of the world, with 133 native species. Of these, 54 have been recorded within the Veragua Rainforest on the Caribbean coast, including the almost ubiquitous red-eye.

Ring-tailed possum
Pseudocheirus peregrinus

WHAT The common ring-tailed possum is a slightly less commonly sighted visitor to Australian backyards than their larger relative the brushtail possum. The tail is the key difference – the ringtail's is prehensile, gripping branches as it moves about the tree canopy. They spend most of their lives above the ground, nesting in dreys with their family. Although ringtails have moved into suburban Australia – where they build their own nest rather than stow away in the roof of a house like the brushtail – they're also widely found in the wild from the top to the bottom of the east coast. You can make a garden more ringtail-friendly by planting native vegetation, installing a hollow log in tree, and keeping cats and dogs indoors after dark.

WHERE At night, shine a torch into trees to look for the reflections of their eyes (or something's eyes). They're widespread in forested areas of national parks and leafy urban parks and gardens.

Ring-tailed lemur
Lemur catta

WHAT With a penchant for group cuddles and sunbathing like blissful yogis, the postures and sociability of this athletic lemur reflects some our own more admirable traits and abilities. It is also a handsome species to behold, moving with balletic grace on two legs, with what might be the most striking tail of any mammal to accentuate every movement.

WHERE Ringtails are restricted to forests and scrublands in the southern half of Madagascar. The numerous troops at Anja Community Reserve on the main southern highway near Fianarantsoa and at Beza Mahafaly Reserve in the southwestern region of Atsimo-Andrefana are wild but habituated to visitors and thus easy to watch and photograph.

© Arto Hakola | Shutterstock

Robin
Erithacus rubecula

WHAT Star of Christmas cards, charming companion to gardeners and often voted Britain's favourite bird, the red-breasted robin has a dark side. Although relaxed around people, the sight of another robin – or even its own reflection – will immediately prompt the avian equivalent of 'oi, what are you looking at?', the puffing of their red-feathered chests, swiftly followed by a fit of violent rage to drive away the interloper. These aggressively territorial birds, part of the chat family, are found in the majority of British gardens, meaning that they're some of the easiest of British birds to spot. And, on the positive side, their spring mating songs are among the prettiest.

WHERE British robins are widespread and not at all shy – look for them in gardens. There are also American robins, part of the thrush family, and very distantly related Australian robins, which have a wider variety of coloured breasts (scarlet, pink and yellow) but similarly aggressive personalities.

Royal albatross *Diomedea sanfordi*

WHAT Albatrosses are the world's largest seabirds, their enormous wingspan an adaptation to flying non-stop for months on end with minimal effort. It takes ten months to rear an albatross chick, so not surprisingly it's a task parent birds only undertake every other year. During the intervening year they cruise the oceans, thousands of miles from land.

WHERE The majority of the world's large albatrosses breed on remote islands (South Georgia, Crozet and other Southern Ocean outposts for the wandering albatross for example), but there is one place you can see them without a major expedition, and it's a must for any wildlife enthusiast visiting New Zealand's South Island. Taiaroa Head (Pukekera) on the Otago Peninsula is home to the only mainland albatross breeding colony in the world – around 60 pairs of northern royal albatross nest here each year.

Saiga *Saiga tatarica*

WHAT One of the world's most critically endangered mammals, the bizarre-looking saiga is a small steppe-dwelling antelope with large eyes and nostrils enlarged into a unique nozzle-like structure that serves to warm the cold steppe air as the animal breathes in and filters dust kicked up by winds or as herds travel en masse. They're odd but appealing creatures, and they have a backstory to break your heart; outbreaks of disease regularly kill tens of thousands of them, and as yet the causes are not fully understood. **WHERE** Several reserves have been created since the 1990s specifically to protect and conserve saiga and their steppe habitat. They include the Altyn Dala National Reserve in Kazakhstan, Chernye Zemli Nature Reserve in the southern Russian republic of Kalmykia, and Shargan and Mankhan in the Gobi-Altai of western Mongolia.

Sailfish
Istiophorus albicans

WHAT If you feel the need for speed, this caped superhero of a fish is guaranteed to satisfy. The sailfish is not only the swiftest of all marine predators, but also one of the most dramatic. The huge dorsal fin for which the species is named is lowered for maximum acceleration, but raised in an instant for tight cornering or to startle and corral prey.

WHERE Winter brings plankton and sardines to the Mexican Caribbean, and where sardines gather, sailfish follow, with numbers peaking from January to March. In many areas you'll be competing with sport fishers keen to hook a trophy, but tight regulations in the waters around the National Park and wildlife reserve of Contoy Island off Cancun allow unparalleled opportunities to snorkel or dive alongside these living torpedoes, and even observe their jaw-dropping hunting behaviour. A closely related species lives in Indo-Pacific waters.

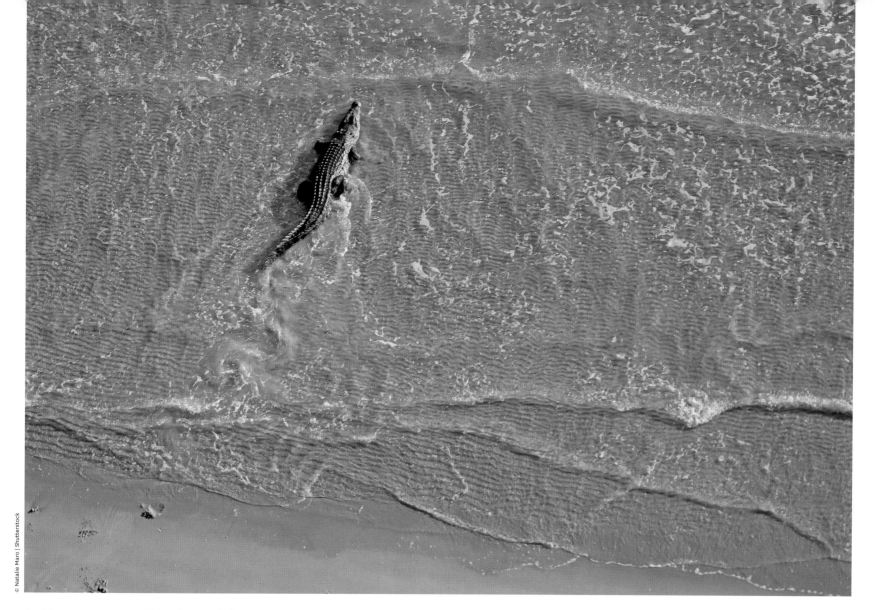

Saltwater crocodile *Crocodylus porosus*

WHAT The world's largest living reptile can exceed 6m in length and weigh well over a tonne. 'Salties' inhabit both fresh and salt water and are able to travel long distances by sea. Despite their prehistoric appearance they are superbly adapted animals – true apex predators, capable of killing and eating virtually any other animal they encounter in the water.

WHERE Salties can be seen in much of Southeast Asia and Oceania, and thrive in Australia's Northern Territories, in particular in the Adelaide, Mary and Daly river systems near Darwin. Crocodile tours have been running on the Adelaide River since the 1970s, and the stars of the show are individuals habituated to tour boats, who leap for meat dangled from poles by experienced tour guides. Fatal attacks on humans are regular, though not common, and almost always take place in shallow water, where the animals can lurk unseen.

THE A-Z OF WILDLIFE WATCHING

Satin bowerbird
Ptilonorhynchus violaceus

WHAT So-called 'land art', in which arrangements of leaves, sand or pebbles form ephemeral works in nature, is seen as a recent artistic movement. But this genius bird has been creating startling natural installations for centuries. Cynics may suggest the mature male bowerbird, himself a vision in violet and black, is stuck in his Blue Period, but the only critic he worries about is the olive and gold female. The twiggy bower he creates is not a nest. She will build that later. No, this is quite simply an exhibition piece, and he adorns the area around it with carefully selected treasures from berries to bottletops, mostly in shades of azure, cobalt and indigo.

WHERE Satin bowerbirds live in the rainforests and sclerophyll forests of eastern Australia. Males and their bowers can sometimes be seen on specialist tours of Lamington National Park, Queensland.

Scarlet macaw *Ara macao*

WHAT Pictures or film footage don't prepare you for the impressive size of this colourful parrot, or for the decibel level at close range. Typical sightings are of one or two birds (they pair for life), flying low over treetops, with their long tails trailing. Their ear-splitting screeches are among the most evocative sounds of their native Amazonia. **WHERE** Scarlet macaws converge in their hundreds at the Chuncho mineral clay licks in the cliffs of the Tambopata river in Peru's Tambopata National Reserve. The licks contain essential salts and chemicals that help neutralise defensive toxins in some of the plants the parrots consume – the birds are in effect self-medicating. The same licks are also frequented by a dozen other parrot species

Scorpion *Pandinus imperator*

WHAT If you want to imagine what life was like on this planet 450 million years ago, check out some scorpions. They've thrived on this flying rock since the Silurian era and their Arachnid family were some of the earliest examples of life on land. As their family name suggests, they're related to spiders (and ticks), possessing eight legs. But scorpions sport a pair of pincers and a tail-mounted stinger for good measure. More than 1500 species exist, of which around 25 have a venom that can kill a human. One of the largest (and thankfully not one of the deadly varieties) is the emperor scorpion of West Africa, which can grow to 20cm in length. **WHERE** Emperor scorpions (above) live in tropical forest and savannah across West Africa, in such countries as Ghana, Guinea, Nigeria, Senegal, Sierrra Leone and Cameroon. Due to their passive nature they're also sold as pets.

Sea otter *Enhydra lutris*

WHAT Sea otters appear to enjoy watching us almost as much as we love observing them. They are inquisitive by nature, with justified confidence in their ability to outmanoeuvre the most agile human visitor to their dominion (they are able to feed, sleep, groom, mate, give birth and nurse young in the water). They perform the essential ecological role of controlling seaweed-eating sea urchins, which almost destroyed the kelp forests that protect Pacific coasts and provide nursery areas for countless other species when the otters were overhunted for their lustrous, waterproof fur coat. Their fur is the thickest of any mammal, with 150,000 hairs per square centimetre. **WHERE** The recovery of sea otters is celebrated from California to Alaska and you can watch them from the shore, from tour boats or from kayaks at places like Big Sur, Elkhorn Slough and Monterey Bay California, and around Vancouver Island in Canada.

THE A-Z OF WILDLIFE WATCHING

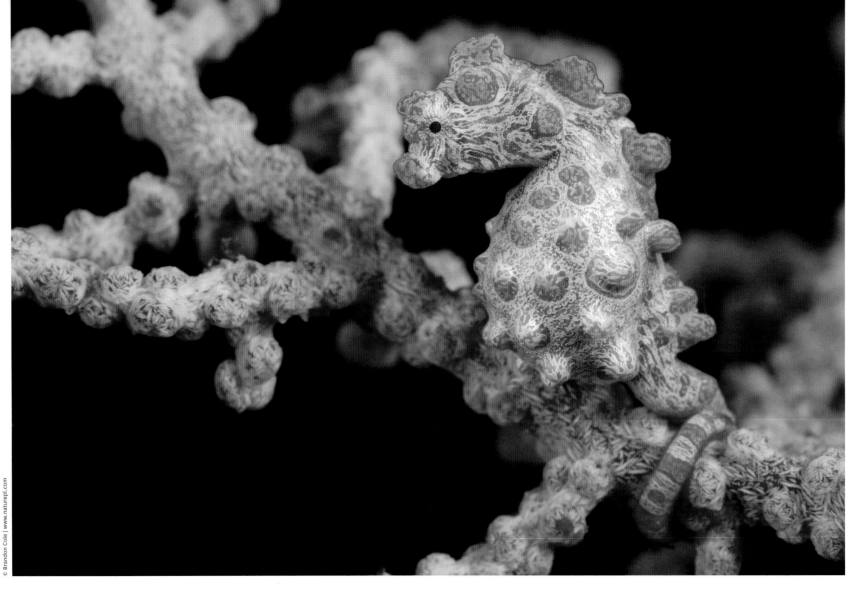

Pygmy seahorses *Hippocampus spp*

WHAT Rapidly becoming a must on every tropical diver's bucket list, these magical little fish are so small and have camouflage so good that most of the eight known species have been discovered only in the last decade. Most are less than 2cm long, some as little as 14mm. They anchor themselves to convenient reef material, usually gorgonian corals, using their prehensile tail, and change colour to suit their surroundings as they wait for planktonic morsels of food to drift by. They're not easy to spot at first, but where you find one, there will likely be several – for fish this small and sedentary, it pays to stay close to others. **WHERE** Dive resorts with good opportunities to spot pygmies include Malapascua, off Cebu in the Philippines, and Wakatobi on Sulawesi. Find a guide to help you get your eye in. And never buy dead seahorses of any species.

Seychelles warbler *Acrocephalus sechellensis*

WHAT In the tropical paradise of the Seychelles, it's easy to overlook a tiny, skulking, olive-brown bird, despite its pretty song. In looks it resembles many of the other members of the warbler family, but the Seychelles warbler is a conservation celebrity. In 1968 only 26 birds survived on Cousin Island, a 34-hectare cartographic speck in the Indian Ocean. The island was made a reserve to protect its precious residents and the population now numbers around 2500 on five islands. The birds are studied intensively by zoologists for their unusual cooperative breeding arrangements, where parent birds are assisted by non-breeding adult female helpers. **WHERE** From Praslin you can take a day-trip to the reserve islands of Cousin and Aride and join a tour led by one of the wardens. Alternatively stay on the resort islands of Cousine, Denis and Frégate, where the warblers also now live.

THE A-Z OF WILDLIFE WATCHING

Shoebill stork
Balaeniceps rex

WHAT This magnificent oddball is a must-have 'tick' for birders visiting East Africa. Previously known as the shoe-billed stork, it is actually a cousin of the pelicans. The bill is among the largest of any bird, and though it looks cumbersome it can be used to lethal effect, the claw-like tip snagging fish prey and the sharp edges capable of decapitating the occasional young crocodile. Shoebills hunt by stealth, waiting poised and motionless until prey comes within range.

WHERE The extensive wetlands of Uganda's Mabamba Swamp offer excellent opportunities to add shoebills to your list, and are in easy striking distance of Kampala, less than 60km away.

© Arterra Picture Library | Alamy Stock Photo

Skylark
Alauda arvensis

WHAT Skylark song is a continuous river of sound without the breaks, or phrasing, typical in most other songbirds. Both males and females can sing, but for territory-holding males it's almost a year-round effort. Their song flights are a show of strength, aimed not only at other larks, but also at impressing predators such as sparrowhawks and merlins, which are less likely to target strong singers. In the breeding season, females pump out up to four clutches of eggs at six week intervals and males go into overdrive, sometimes beginning to sing as early as 3am.

WHERE The ultimate spine-tingling skylark experience is 'lark rise': the first song of the day, delivered in pre-dawn darkness. The first Sunday in May is International Dawn Chorus Day – as good a time as any to take advantage of guided walks and events in areas of mixed grassland and moor such as the Yorkshire Moors and Dales, and the Pembrokeshire and Exmoor National Parks in Britain.

Slate pencil urchin
Heterocentrotus mamillatus

WHAT It may look more like a clockwork desk toy or a WWII mine, but this eccentric invertebrate is an echinoderm – a cousin of sea stars and sea cucumbers. It has no brain, no front or back end, just a coil of gut and voluminous gonads inside a shell-like case, the test. Unlike other urchins, whose spines are narrow, needle-sharp and defensive, its spines are modified into pencil-thick radiols, whose main function is to help wedge the animal into rock crevices. **WHERE** The pencil urchins of Hawaii have a distinctive red colouring. A little effort exploring reefs such as those at French Frigate Shoals will give you a sighting of the animal itself and maybe a few of its 'pencils' – a far better souvenir than anything you might buy.

© ArteSub | Alamy Stock Photo

Snow leopard *Panthera uncia*

WHAT Author Peter Matthiessen spends the whole extent of his book *The Snow Leopard* in search of the snow leopard, 'whose terrible beauty is the very stuff of human longing.' It is, he thinks, 'the animal I would most like to be eaten by.' It is easy to see why: wild snow leopards live above us mortals, blending into the snow and rock of the mountains of central Asia and the Himalaya. They hunt wild sheep and goats in this precipitous environment with unparalleled skill and grace, using their long, thick tails for balance. Slowly we're learning more about these big cats and local communities are beginning to conserve and not kill them. But it is estimated that there are around just 5000 remaining. **WHERE** In Ladakh, India, snow leopards are known to inhabit Hemis National Park. For the best chance of one of the world's rarest wildlife experiences visit in winter, employ local guides and stay in Rumbak Valley. And read *The Snow Leopard* (no spoilers).

Snowy owl *Bubo scandiacus*

WHAT Despite its grumpy expression, this has owl a lot going for it: showstopping good looks, stature rivalling that of an eagle owl, and, thanks to JK Rowling, global recognition. Most are seasonal migrants, but influxes to wintering grounds in southern Canada and northern US vary greatly depending on the population cycles of lemming prey further north, which fluctuate on a six to nine-year cycle. **WHERE** If you have deep pockets and a yen for Arctic wildlife in general, Wrangel Island on the coast of Siberia has it all, including the largest population of breeding snowies. Wintering birds require less of an expedition but the best places vary from year to year. They are often drawn to the tundra-like expanses of airports such as Boston and Montreal, to the consternation of safety authorities. For more natural photo opportunities the protected marshlands of Boundary Bay Regional Park in British Columbia are a good bet.

Sociable weaver
Philetairus socius

WHAT The chief wonder of this species is perhaps not the bird itself – a relatively drab 'little brown job', as birders describe many species of small brown passerine birds – but its extraordinary home. While other weaver species build nests seasonally for breeding, the sociable weaver occupies its nest year-round, and shares it with up to 400 neighbours. The largest nests resemble haystacks assembled miraculously around the branches of a tree or electricity pole, and some are many decades old. The arrangement is not entirely communal, because each pair has its own chamber and front door, much like human families sharing an apartment block. Look closely – some residents are not weavers at all, but opportunist lodgers such as the pygmy falcon.

WHERE Sociable weavers area restricted to northern South Africa, Namibia and Botswana. They are abundant in reserves such as Tswalu Kalahari and the Kgalagadi Transfrontier Park.

Sockeye salmon *Oncorhynchus nerka*

WHAT The strange name 'sockeye' comes from suk-kegh meaning 'red fish' in the First Nation Halkomelem language, and in early summer some rivers of western North America turn crimson with the bodies of these hugely impressive fish as they return from the Pacific to spawn in the places they were hatched. It's a gargantuan effort that invariably costs them their lives. **WHERE** Redfish Lake in Idaho is 2000m above sea level, 1500km inland up the Snake River and separated from the sea by several hydroelectric dams. And yet the fish that earned the lake its name still battle the odds the odds to spawn here, boosted by recent conservation measures. Elsewhere, such fish returning in greater numbers face another challenge – a gauntlet of anglers keen to pit their skills against this hard-fighting quarry. The species is celebrated by an annual festival on the Adams River in British Columbia.

Southern carmine bee-eater *Merops nubicoides*

WHAT Like a vividly coloured hallucination, waves of these large scarlet bee-eaters pulse through the African air pursuing insects – not just bees but locusts, flies, dragonflies and butterflies. Their annual journey to nesting sites is one of the continent's most spectacular migrations. Appropriately, for their plumage, they've been known to fly close to bush fires, picking off the insects flushed out by the flames. **WHERE** From August, southern carmine bee-eaters arrive on the Luangwa River in South Luangwa National Park in eastern Zambia to breed. They mate, nest and raise their chicks here for about three months before dispersing again. The park can be reached by car from Chipata or by air via Mfuwe airport.

Southern elephant seal
Mirounga leonina

WHAT With adult males weighing anything up to 5000kg, this is by far the world's largest furry carnivore. Bulls are five or more times heavier than even the largest females, which appear at first sight to belong to an entirely different species. The males have attitude to match their bulk, using size and roaring bravado to intimidate most rivals. When this fails, fighting breaks out and the victor gains control of breeding beaches and harems of females. Lower-ranked bulls often loiter off-shore, calling to females to join them for illicit matings in the water.

WHERE Non-breeding elephant seals can be encountered throughout southern polar and temperate oceans, but between August and November the action moves closer to land. Most breeding beaches are on remote islands, with South Georgia home to half the world population. Argentina's Valdès peninsula boasts the only breeding site on a continental mainland.

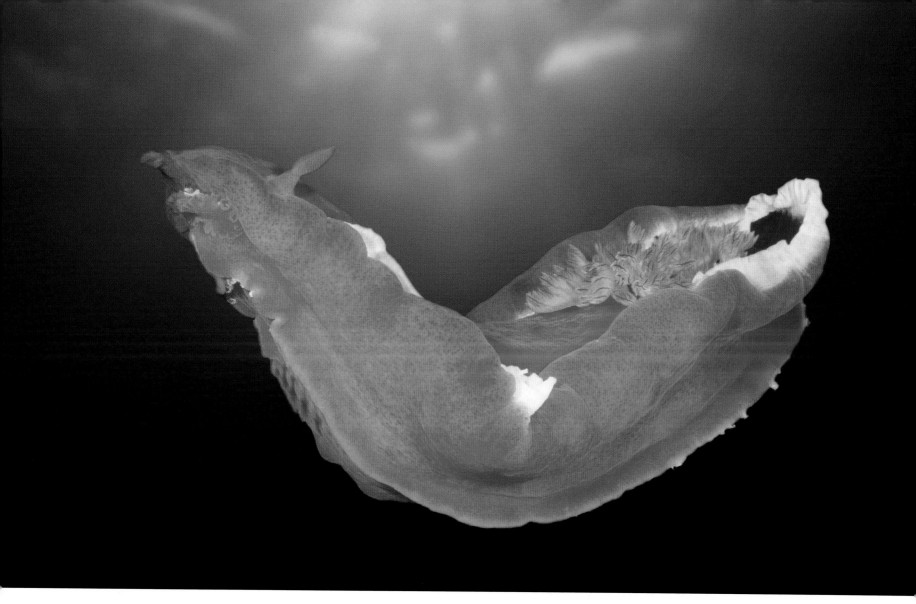

Spanish dancer nudibranch *Morus bassanus*

WHAT This creeping reef-dweller is a slug – a shell-less gastropod mollusc – but what a slug! Not only is it floridly colourful (a warning of toxicity), it is the largest of its kind, growing up to 60cm. It feeds mainly on the sponges and tunicate colonies over which it crawls. But the real drama unfolds if the slug is disturbed, when a 'skirt' that is normally rolled around the edges of the body unfurls, and the animal flings itself into the water with wild undulations of the body. Call it swimming, call it dancing – it's a spectacle. As a bonus, look out for the tiny emperor shrimp, which often lives around the slug, gathering fragments of dislodged food. **WHERE** You can dive or snorkel with the Spanish dancer on reefs throughout much of the tropical and subtropical Indo-Pacific and Red Sea.

THE A-Z OF WILDLIFE WATCHING

Sparrowhawk
Accipiter nisus

WHAT What the diminutive sparrowhawk lacks in stature – it's one of Europe's smallest hawks – it more than makes up for with intensity, agility and ferocity. When fixed with a piercing stare from its large yellow eyes, any of the 120 species of bird on which it preys in Britain will have good cause to fear for its life. Sparrowhawks are often seen pursuing prey in fast-moving dogfights around Britain's gardens. The much larger female hawks are able to take a pigeon but males are limited to thrushes or smaller birds. The young sparrowhawks have brown plumage before maturing into the grey and white bars of the adults (males have a russet hue to their chest). **WHERE** In Britain, aside from gardens, they can be spotted in the Royal Society for the Protection of Birds' reserves at Blean Woods, Bowers Marsh and Wolves Wood.

Sperm whale *Physeter macrocephalus*

WHAT The largest active predator on earth, the deepest diving mammal, the largest brained animal – sperm whales hold more than their share of record-breaking statistics. The species can also claim cult literary status as the eponymous star of Herman Melville's classic American novel Moby Dick. **WHERE** For decades, the small coastal town of Kaikōura on the east coast of New Zealand's South Island has been synonymous with whale watching, and sperm whales are by far the most reliable large species, thanks to the proximity of the 3000m-deep Kaikōura Channel to land. The deep water is home to plentiful large squid, the sperm whale's main prey. Males are present here all year, while other whales using the area include humpbacks, minkes, southern rights, blues, various beaked species and dolphins.

THE A-Z OF WILDLIFE WATCHING

Spider crab (giant)
Leptomithrax gaimardii

WHAT This magnificent crustacean is one of several related species found in oceans around the world. The largest is the Japanese spider crab, with a leg span up to 5.5m, but it lives in such deep water that the only realistic chance of seeing one alive is in an aquarium. But size isn't everything, and this Australian cousin offers something else – a spectacle of numbers. Each winter, hundreds of thousands of crabs march over the seabed and converge in their multitudes in shallow water off Melbourne. Here, in the relative safely of huge numbers, they cast off their armoured exoskeleton, allowing the new larger one growing beneath to harden.

WHERE Several Melbourne dive operators offer trips to view the annual crabfest in Port Phillip Bay from May to July. The huge numbers around Rye Pier and Blairgowrie Pier on the Mornington Peninsula can also be seen from the beach or by donning a snorkel.

Spider monkey
Ateles geoffroyi

WHAT Spider monkeys are swingers not leapers, using their long limbs and prehensile tails to swing through the trees of Latin America. Of the various species, one of the most endangered is Geoffroy's spider monkey, which lives along the Central American isthmus from Mexico to Panama. It is one of the largest and most charismatic of New World monkeys, measuring 30-60cm in length. They live in large matriarchal family groups of 20 to 40 individuals, foraging for fruit in smaller packs.

WHERE The Osa Peninsula, in Costa Rica's southwest, is the most inaccessible and rugged corner of the country but it's also the most biodiverse and is where Geoffroy's spider monkeys can still be sighted (with jaguars and harpy eagles that prey on them). Here, Corcovado National Park is large reserve of lowland tropical rainforest best accessed via Drake Bay or Puerto Jimenez. Dry season is November to April.

Spinner dolphin
Stenella longirostris

WHAT While most dolphins breach from time to time, the long-beaked or spinner dolphins have elevated leaping to a dizzying performance art. Not only do they leap higher than most – achieving up to 3m clearance from the water – they manage to incorporate anything up to seven full rotations of the body before crashing back down. Explanations for the behaviour abound, but most likely it functions in communication. Spinners are highly gregarious, with groups sometimes merging into superpods of 1000 or more. They are also enthusiastic bow-wave riders, often accompanying boats for miles, seemingly just for fun.

WHERE Spinners are present year-round off Hawaii, with many well known pods in easy reach of tour boats. But be careful – recent research suggests that regular disturbance may be detrimental to the animals, which hunt nocturnally and come to nearshore waters to rest after hunting.

© Lindsay Fendt | Alamy Stock Photo

Spirit bear
Ursus americanus kermodei

WHAT Wait a minute. Is that a polar bear in a rain forest? You'd be forgiven for doing a double-take. But look past the white coat at the shape of the head and the large ears and you might see that this is in fact an American black bear, roughly half the size of its Arctic cousin. Spirit bears are a subspecies of black bear, generally restricted to British Columbia, in which roughly 10% have the double recessive gene for a white coat. Unsurprisingly the trait has lead to a rich folklore among First Nation peoples and to the development of a low-key ecotourism industry. On the bears themselves, it confers an advantage when fishing, serving to camouflage them against a light sky.

WHERE Spirit bears are restricted to Central and Northern British Columbia, including the aptly named Great Bear Rainforest.

© Wendy Shattil | Alamy Stock Photo

Spitting cobra
Naja ashei

WHAT If there's one reptile to give a wide berth, it's any of the spitting cobra species of Asia and Africa. Specifically, you'll need to be at least 2m away – or be wearing eye protection. These cobras have demonstrated incredible accuracy when spitting venom and can hit their target – your eyes – at least 80% of the time. The largest of the spitting cobras lives in East Africa, in the lowlands of eastern Kenya also in parts of Somalia, Ethiopia and Uganda. It's a substantial snake that can grow to in excess of 2m in length (though would still be dwarfed by the 5m king cobra of India). **WHERE** In Kenya, this large species of spitting cobra has been found in Tsavo East National Park, 250km south of Nairobi. It's not the only dangerous snake in the park: there are also puff adders, responsible for most of Africa's snakebites, and the very deadly (but quite shy) boomslang.

© Mariette Vogel | Shutterstock

Spotted hyena *Crocuta crocuta*

WHAT Perhaps the most unfairly maligned of all mammals, the reputation of spotted hyenas as skulking hermaphrodite freeloaders dates back almost two millennia to the writings of Pliny the Elder. But spend a bit of time watching these super-intelligent social operators and you'll see plenty of hunting and other highly organised and co-operative behaviour. Females are socially dominant and typically 10% heavier than males, but difficult to recognise because of their unique and conspicuous genitals, which look very much like a penis.

WHERE Spotted hyenas remain widespread across Sub-Saharan Africa, and most wildlife tours in the region will offer good opportunities to see them. To follow the footsteps of the celebrated zoologist Hans Kruuk, whose studies did much to illuminate their extraordinary lives, head for the National Parks of Ngorongoro Crater and Serengeti in Tanzania.

THE A-Z OF WILDLIFE WATCHING

Springbok
Antidorcas marsupialis

WHAT The animal symbol of South Africa is a medium-sized antelope with a big personality. In their signature behaviour, animals spring repeatedly into the air on straight legs, catapulted by highly elastic tendons. These bouts of so-called 'pronking' (from an Afrikaans verb meaning 'to show off') may be triggered by the threat of a predator or by social cues.

WHERE The vast nation-sized Kgalagadi Transfrontier Park lies wholly within the sparsely vegetated, arid expanse of the Kalahari Desert between South Africa and Botswana. Though the species is far less numerous here than in the past, when herds numbering hundreds of thousands took days to pass through the area on migrations known as trebokken, it continues to be a good place to see them. Further south, the species can also be seen on game farms breeding animals for hunting.

Starling *Sturnus vulgaris*

WHAT Ever-shifting and changing shape, murmurations are one of the natural world's most mesmerising spectacles. They are flocks of thousands of starlings, flying in unison each winter evening in locations across Europe before settling to roost. The reasons for this display are not fully understood – to dissuade predators, share dining tips, keep warm or just for the kicks. In North America starlings are an invasive and problematic species. Just 100 birds were released in Central Park in New York City in the 1890s by Eugene Schieffelin, who had the misguided notion of introducing all the birds mentioned in William Shakespeare's plays to North America. **WHERE** Murmurations can be witnessed from West Cork in Ireland (at Timoleague) to, famously, Rome, where a million starlings may congregrate from November onwards. Several of the RSPB's reserves in Britain host murmurations too. Look to the skies at dusk.

Starry sky pufferfish *Torquigener albomaculosus*

WHAT This unassuming puffer captured the hearts and imagination of scientists and armchair nature lovers alike when it was identified in 2014 as the architect of mysterious structures on sandy seabeds in Japan's southern Ryukyu archipelago. Compared to 'undersea crop circles', the designs are among the most complex structures built by any animal. Male starry sky puffers create them to showcase their quality to passing females, much as bower birds construct decorative arenas. Like most other puffers, it can inflate its body when alarmed, and its flesh is highly toxic. **WHERE** The seas around the island of Amami Ōshima 300km south of Kyushu are a popular dive area, with reefs and the sandy beds favoured by starry sky puffers. Males usually nest between 15m and 25m down, within reach of recreational divers.

Steller's sea eagle *Haliaeetus pelagicus*

WHAT This battleaxe of a bird is the largest and most photogenic of the fish eagles. Females reach a massive 9kg, with a wingspan up to 2.5m. The contrasting near-black and brilliant white plumage of both sexes couldn't be more dramatic – even in low light. Add the strident yellow of the enormous fish-shredding bill and powerful feet, and a minimalist backdrop of icebound sea, and you have a photographer's dream. **WHERE** These magnificent birds breed principally on Russia's Kamchatka Peninsula, but they are more easily viewed in their Japanese wintering areas, in particular the Nemuro Peninsula on the northeast coast of Hokkaido where the coastal wetland of Lake Furen is good for roosting birds. Better still, take an early morning boat from Rausu in early February to see them fishing for Pacific cod at amazingly close quarters among the ice floes of the Nemuro Strait.

THE A-Z OF WILDLIFE WATCHING

Straw-coloured fruit bat *Eidolon helvum*

WHAT This is certainly not the only bat to occur in flocks of more than a million, but it is the largest, with individual wingspans of up to a metre. The flight style is a highly efficient flap-flap-glide, allowing the species to travel further in a year than any other African mammal, in search of seasonal foods like fruits, buds and shoots. They also chew wood to suck out sap and their sometimes destructive feeding habits are balanced by their role as pollinators. **WHERE** Straw-coloureds may be the most widely distributed and far ranging large bats in Africa, but to see the spectacle for which the species is becoming best known, head to tiny Kasanka National Park in Zambia, where an estimated five million bats arrive from the Democratic Republic of Congo each year and roost in a few acres of forest.

Lake sturgeon
Acipenser spp

WHAT Around 24 living species of these huge, slow-growing and appropriately prehistoric-looking fish are known from rivers and lakes and coasts of Eurasia and North America. Some were once so abundant as to be regarded as worthless nuisance species – until a preposterous increase in the value of caviar (sturgeon eggs, or roe) threatened them all with extinction. **WHERE** The colossal beluga sturgeon of the Black and Caspian Sea basins has become vanishingly rare. Current efforts to establish sustainable farming offer some hope of recovery, with the tantalising prospect of sturgeon tourism in ancestral spawning rivers such as the Volga, the Ural and the Kura. Until then, the best prospects of a sighting are of the smaller North American lake sturgeon, native to Great Lakes catchments. With luck in early summer fish can be seen preparing to spawn in shallow nearshore waters or entering adjoining rivers. Hatcheries established to boost native stocks occasionally hold public open days.

Sugar glider
Petaurus breviceps

WHAT Sugar (mostly in the form of sweet plant sap and nectar) is an important food for these appealing marsupials, though they also eat a wide range of other foods, including copious insects. They forage nocturnally, almost exclusively in forest canopies, and deploy gliding to travel efficiently from tree to tree. The gliding membrane is a web of super-stretchy, furry skin connecting the front and back legs. Glides of up to 50m are known, with the horizontal distance usually up to 1.8 times the vertical distance fallen.

WHERE The rainforest-clad mountains and tablelands of Northern Queensland have gliders galore – six species in total, including the tiny feathertails and rare mahogany gliders as well as sugar gliders. Crater Lakes National Park on the Atherton Tablelands is a good bet – tourist lodges such as those at Lake Eacham often erect feeding stations for their sweet-toothed nocturnal visitors.

Sun bear
Helarctos malayanus

WHAT This is the smallest of the world's bears, with a weight range similar to that of humans, and a similar set of 'bear necessities'. Sun bears have no need to hibernate given that their preferred foods are available year-round. They consume large quantities of honey and insects, in particular bees, ants and termites, topped up with ripe fruit, eggs, small vertebrate prey and carrion – much the same foods we'd select from a tropical forest habitat. But there the Jungle Book analogies end – unlike the fictional Baloo, sun bears are decidedly grumpy so treat them with extreme respect.

WHERE Sun bears have a patchy distribution across much of Southeast Asia, including the Malay Peninsula and the large islands of Sumatra and Borneo. Rehabilitated individuals can be seen in natural habitat at the Bornean Sun Bear Conservation Centre in Sandakan, Sabah.

Giant sunfish *Mola mola*

WHAT As a tall fin breaks the surface, your first thought might be 'shark'. But wait – the fin is tilting slowly, drunkenly to one side, and as it topples something huge appears at the surface, and it's unlike anything else in the ocean. Where the body should be, there is just a gigantic goggle-eyed head, and behind the head, a weird knobbly tail – no wonder this strange apparition seems to have difficulty swimming. In fact it is basking – rewarming the body before descending to cool deep water, where it swims steadily, if not fast, after slow-moving prey, mainly jellyfish. At up to 1.8m long, 2.5m tall and 1000kg in weight, the ocean sunfish is the world's heaviest bony fish, with few natural predators to fear.

WHERE Ocean sunfish live in tropical and temperate oceans worldwide. At Nusa Lembongan and Nusa Penida off Bali these mysterious giants can be seen visiting reefs to use the services of the cleaner fish that feed on the dead skin, parasites and other things growing on the bodies of bigger fish.

© Sompreaw | Shutterstock

© A Life Beneath Stars | Shutterstock

Superb fairywren *Malurus cyaneus*

WHAT A tiny, iridescent blue jewel hops from the bush to the path in front of you to snatch a fly then flits back to the undergrowth. It's a male superb fairywren, a much-loved Australian bird and one of eleven colourful wren species in Australia and New Guinea (including the lovely fairywren and the splendid fairywren). It is not, however, a member of the Old World wren family. Males develop the blue plumage during the breeding season. But there's a cost to the bold colouration: female fairywrens, safe in their brown outfits, may admire the brightest males but they're also more visible to predators. Who dares wins... **WHERE** The wrens are common along the east coast of Victoria, New South Wales and southern Queensland and are often sighted in towns and suburbs wherever there is plant cover.

Swift
Apus apus

WHAT Arcing through the summer sky, shrieking with what must be sheer pleasure, the swift brings joy to anybody watching their high-speed acrobatics from below. There's no more welcome sight in northern countries than the arrival of the first swifts, which migrate from Africa to breed each summer. The swift's scythe-shaped wings are perfect for flying, which is just as well because they spend most of their lives in the air, even sleeping on the wing. One swift was recorded covering 5000km of its migration from Liberia to the UK in just five days. They nest under eaves but find it harder each year to source suitable sites. Then, less than three months after their arrival, they head back to Africa every August. **WHERE** In 2017, Oxford became the UK's first Swift City, a RSPB initiative to encourage swift-friendly features. So, watch for them wheeling about the city's spires in June and July.

© Markus Varesvuo | www.naturepl.com

Takahē
Porphyrio hochstetteri

WHAT On an elegantly proportioned bird, gleaming green and blue plumage and a gaudy red beak and legs could be showstopping, but on this portly, flightless coot-cousin, the effect is more eccentric than glamorous. Nevertheless, a sighting of New Zealand's South Island takahē is a memory to treasure, especially since the species was thought extinct in the early 20th century. **WHERE** Takahē can be seen easily at the Te Anau Bird Sanctuary, and on predator-free island reserves including Maud, Mana, Kapiti and Tirititi Matangi. For a less canned experience you could trek into the nearby Murchison Mountains, where the species was rediscovered in 1948 and still exists in small numbers, though there's no guarantee of a sighting. Perhaps more accessible is the tussocky grassland of the Gouland Downs in Kahurangi National Park near Nelson. Here you may spot recently reintroduced takahē from the 80km (4-6 day) Heaphy walking track.

© Artush | Shutterstock

© Adrian Hepworth | Alamy Stock Photo

Tapir (Baird's) *Tapirus bairdii*

WHAT The largest of the three New World tapir species (the piebald Malayan tapir is larger still) is also the largest wild animal you'll see in Central America. A gentle herbivore, it browses using its odd prehensile snout to pluck leaves and shoots. **WHERE** Baird's tapir is the national animal of Belize, and you'd be forgiven for thinking Tapir Mountain would be the place to go to see it. In fact the reserve here is not open to the public, though adjoining land may be a good place to look. There are more accessible populations in neighbouring Costa Rica, though luck is always needed to spot these unpredictable animals. Corcovado National Park is a good bet, with early mornings providing the best opportunities, so plan to stay overnight at Sirena Ranger Station and book a guided hike.

© Haveseen | Shutterstock

© Artush Foto | 500px

Tarsier *Tarsiidae spp*

WHAT The world's second smallest primate (about 15cm in length) has a branch of its own in our family tree and these ancient ancestors have remained relatively unchanged over the last 45 million years. They're the only completely carnivorous primates, feasting on insects (and occasionally birds and small reptiles) that they hunt at night using what are the largest eyes for their body size of any mammal. However, being unable to move their enormous ocular equipment they have had to evolve the ability to rotate their heads 180 degrees. **WHERE** Species of tarsier live across a swathe of Southeast Asian islands, including the Philippines and Malaysia. In 2008 the pygmy tarsier was rediscovered on the Indonesian island of Sulawesi, having been thought to be extinct. In Indonesia, Tangkoko-Batuangas Dua Saudara Nature Reserve is an accessible home to tarsiers. You can take tours there from across North Sulawesi. Batuputih is the gateway town.

THE A-Z OF WILDLIFE WATCHING

Tasmanian devil *Sarcophilus harrisii*

WHAT An unearthly yowling shocks onlookers: it's feeding time at the Tasmanian Devil sanctuary and the small black creature making the hellish screams is chasing its companion – which carries a large bone in its jaws – around their compound. These are Australia's Tasmanian devils, terrier-sized balls of fury that are, with the extinction of the thylacine, Tasmania's apex predator. Or rather scavenger; these primitive marsupials have evolved bone-cracking jaws and are more likely to eat roadkill than hunt a wallaby. Their aggressive nature doesn't help them face their greatest threat, a facial tumour disease that is transmitted by biting – about 95% of the wild devil population died from 1996 to 2015.

WHERE Devils are far harder to see in the wild these days (although always watch out along roadsides at dusk). But the Tasmanian Devil Conservation Park on the road to Port Arthur has several from which disease-free devils are being bred.

Tawny frogmouth
Podargus strigoides

WHAT If you've ever noticed a fence post slowly open its eyes, you've probably seen a tawny frogmouth, a unique owl-like Australian bird that is a master of disguise. They're nocturnal hunters, feeding on insects, worms and occasionally frogs or small birds. But they're hard to spot, their mottled plumage blending into tree trunks perfectly. Frogmouths – a family of about 14 species – are not owls but are more closely related to nightjars. During the day they will hide among branches and if disturbed will stiffen their bodies to resemble wood, a behaviour called 'stumping'. **WHERE** Tawny frogmouths are widespread across most Australian states, petering out in northern Queensland and the Northern Territory. Keep your eyes peeled in woodland and scrub, but they especially favour roadsides, drawn by the insects that are attracted to the beams of car headlights – a dangerous hunting strategy for the frogmouth.

Termites (magnetic) *Amitermes meridionalis*

WHAT While termites themselves are interesting to entomologists, for most of us it's their architecture that captivates. Over hundreds or thousands of generations, these prodigious builders construct fortresses exceeding anything built by humans in terms of relative scale. Termites are highly social insects, related to cockroaches, though in appearance and in their highly organised cooperative societies they more closely resemble ants, with different individuals specialising in roles such as defence, foraging or breeding. Their mounds contain labyrinthine tunnels, nurseries and chambers where fungi are farmed on rotting plant matter brought in by the army of workers. This particular species builds wedged-shaped mounds up to 4m high and aligned north-south, so that they are warmed by morning and evening sun, but not blasted by fierce midday rays. **WHERE** Magnetic termites are a speciality of Australia's Northern Territories, with several large groups resembling standing stones or gravestones in the north of Litchfield National Park.

Thorny devil *Moloch horridus*

WHAT This charismatic desert dweller is a rare thing – an exciting but harmless Australian reptile. The spiny body ornamentation serves not only in self-defence and camouflage but also to channel precious water condensing on the body to the mouth via microscopic grooves. Check out the bulbous structure on the back of the neck – it's a false head, used as a decoy if the devil is threatened, while the real one is tucked away out of harm's way. When the coast is clear, the devil moves off again, often using an eccentric rocking gait, as though grooving to music only it can hear. **WHERE** Thorny devils are native to Central and Western Australia and can be spotted in the tourist hotspot of Uluru-Kata Tjuta National Park. If you don't get lucky there, a small number live semi-wild at the nearby Alice Springs Desert Park.

THE A-Z OF WILDLIFE WATCHING

Three-toed sloth *Bradypus variegatus*

WHAT Costa Ricans love their sloths, and you'll see sloth images everywhere, including on the currency. But given the size of this species and its total inability to run away you might be surprised to discover how elusive these famously sluggish mammals can be. In fact, it's possible to be within just a couple of metres of one and not realise. Not only does it spend most of its time motionless and high above head height, but its shaggy grizzled fur is often tinted green by algae cultivated in the hollow hair shafts, providing effective camouflage.

WHERE The Sloth Sanctuary on the Caribbean coast is home to both Costa Rica's native sloths, the other being Hoffmann's two-toed sloth. Sanctuary tours include a canoe trip on which wild sloths can be spotted from the river.

© MaViLa| Getty images

Tiger (Bengal)
Panthera tigris tigris

WHAT Is there anything more intense in the natural world than a tiger? It's hard to imagine a 200kg killing machine more supple, more athletic, or more downright beautiful. The expanding population in India is a source of optimism and pride, and ethical tiger tourism has a huge role to play. The Bengal tiger is the most numerous of several sub-species. The memory of the world's largest cat reclining in a glade, bathing, patrolling a dirt road with lazy confidence or threading through trees to vanish in a moment will last a lifetime. **WHERE** Perhaps the best chances of a sighting are in Bandhavgarh National Park in Madhya Pradesh, with the famous (and busier) Ranthambore National Park in Rajasthan a close second. In both, tigers are accustomed to visitors. Other areas may have larger or denser populations, for example the Sundarbans, but the swampy terrain will limit your chances – travelling is difficult, tiger hiding places abound, and yes, some of them are man-eaters.

Tree kangaroo
Dendrolagus spp

WHAT Most macropods – the family that includes kangaroos and wallabies – are happiest hopping around on the ground. Not the tree kangaroo. This idiosyncratic relative has returned to the trees, evolving longer forelimbs and shorter legs for a life less bouncy. There are 14 species of tree kangaroo, two of which live in Australia (the Bennett's and Lumholtz's), the rest on New Guinea where the Wandiwoi tree kangaroo is thought to number as few as 50. In 1990 a new species of tree kangaroo was discovered: the golden-mantled tree kangaroo, with populations on both sides of New Guinea. It joins Matschie's tree kangaroo (right), which resides on the Huon peninsula in the 4000m peaks of its cloud-forest-covered mountains.

WHERE With the help of Seattle's Woodland Park Zoo and its Tree Kangaroo Conservation Program, YUS Conservation Area of northeast Papua New Guinea – the country's first – brings together land around 50 villages and enlists indigenous people to help protect the region's incredible biodiversity, including the tree kangaroo. Yawan is a village at the centre of the Conversation Area.

Tuatara *Sphenodon punctatus*

WHAT There's a special kind of mindfulness to be achieved by staring into the unblinking gaze of a living, breathing fossil. Breathing is something tuataras do only once or twice an hour. They grow slowly too – taking 30 years to reach full size and breeding only once every four or five years. This way of life served them well in New Zealand before the introduction of rats and cats, from which they must now be rigorously protected. Despite appearances, tuataras are not lizards, but the sole survivors of a group more than 200 million years old.

WHERE Most islands with tuatara have no-landing rules to avoid the accidental transfer of rats, but you can visit Matiu/Somes Island in Wellington Harbour and Tiritiri-Matangi Island near Auckland, where there are strict bag-search policies. The only place to see free-living tuatara on the mainland is Zealandia in Wellington, where a 9km-fence keeps predators out.

THE A-Z OF WILDLIFE WATCHING

Uakari
Cacajao calvus

WHAT This extraordinary Amazonian monkey resembles a miniature orang-utan, with shaggy auburn hair and a short, almost non-existent tail. But the similarity ends at the neckline, leaving a bald head with what looks like an appalling case of sunburn. The oddness is compounded in dominant males by dual swellings at the temples that lend a distinctive 'butthead' appearance. In fact the glowing red face and pate are a badge of health, since paler individuals are likely to be suffering from malaria. Uakaris are treetop specialists of frequently flooded forests. Their complex sociality is only beginning to be understood.

WHERE The vast Mamirauá Sustainable Development Reserve in Brazil is one of the most strictly protected areas of Amazonia. If your budget runs to it, the floating Uakari Lodge there is named with good reason. Or try Reserva Natural Zacambú near Leticia on the Peruvian side of Río Zacambú, part of the Yavarí Basin, a stronghold for the species.

© Ingo Arndt | www.naturepl.com

© Cyril Ruoso | www.naturepl.com

Vicuña *Vicugna vicugna*

WHAT This dainty alpine ungulate is the smallest of the camel and llama family, and is regarded as a living treasure in Peru, thanks to its exquisitely fine, warm fleece. By weight vicuña wool is one of the world's most valuable textiles. A vicuña scarf will set you back up to $1500, but beware the black market in illegally harvested wool. The current population of more than 300,000 animals is in good shape compared to the 6000 that survived in the 1970s, but dependent on conservation and strict regulation of trade. **WHERE** The greatest density of vicuña is to be seen in Pampa Galeras-Barbara D'Achille National Park, near Nazca. In the annual government-sanctioned Chaku (or Chaccu) fiesta on 24 June, animals are rounded up for shearing, with individuals shorn no more than once in three years to ensure their welfare.

Walrus *Odobenus rosmarus*

WHAT This huge Arctic seal-cousin hunts by touch using its moustache of wiry bristles and feeds by suction powerful enough to open large clams. The tusks, too long to be any use in feeding, serve as grappling hooks when the walrus pulls itself from the water onto ice floes, giving rise to the scientific name *odobenus*, meaning 'toothwalker'.

WHERE The remote sites favoured by walrus make them an expensive bucket list tick, but haulouts such as those on Cape Seniavin and Round Island in western Alaska are well serviced by tour operators, with options for single- or multi-day trips by air from Anchorage. In Europe, a high-summer trip to the abandoned mining settlement of Pyramiden on Spitzbergen offers good opportunities to see the slightly smaller Atlantic variety.

© Jo Crebbin | Shutterstock

Waxwing *Bombycilla garrulus/spp*

WHAT These exquisitely coiffed birds appear to be clothed in silk and adorned with curls of crimson and gold wax. These intense flecks of colour are derived from pigments in fruit the birds consume avidly for much of the year. In winter individuals can devour several hundreds of berries a day, more than double their body weight. They feed communally and the sight of a hungry flock recently arrived from the north in early winter and feeding among fruit-laden branches of rowan, hawthorn, holly and yew is a highlight of the birding calendar in temperate Europe. **WHERE** Waxwing eruptions (large-scale movements in search of winter food) are, literally, a moveable feast, with birds arriving, stripping fruit and moving on within days or even hours. The best bet is to familiarise yourself with locations offering suitable berry trees, check regularly and use social media to alert you to arrivals.

THE A-Z OF WILDLIFE WATCHING

Wētāpunga
Deinacrida heteracantha

WHAT With its Maori name meaning 'God of ugly things' the wētāpunga is the largest of New Zealand's formidable cricket-like wētās, and one of the world's largest insects, with females easily outweighing an average sparrow or mouse. Despite appearances, they are leaf-eating herbivores.

WHERE Described as the 'jewel in the crown' of New Zealand conservation, Hauturu-o-Toi or Little Barrier Island lies 80km north of Auckland. Giant wētās are among many hundreds of threatened species of animal and plant that survived here after being extirpated on the mainland. Visits require a permit from the Department of Conservation and are subject to strict biosecurity – be prepared to have bags and clothing searched for stowaways. The species was reintroduced to Motuora island on 2010 and Tiritiri Matangi island in 2011.

© Mark Carwardine | www.naturepl.com

Whale shark *Rhincodon typus*

WHAT At up to 12.6m and 21 tonnes, the world's largest fish has a vast global range, occurring almost anywhere with ocean temperatures higher than 21°C. A filter feeder, it cruises at around five kilometres an hour – a speed that can be matched by humans for short distances. Individual sharks appear tolerant of company and the shark-watching industry is booming in areas where large numbers gather seasonally. Try to avoid tours where sharks are fed, as this disrupts their natural behaviour, and resist the temptation to touch or approach close than 5m – it's a shark, not a fairground ride. **WHERE** In July and August, Cancun, Mexico is whale shark central. Highly regulated tours around the islands of Holbox, Contoy and Mujeres often guarantee sightings. Swimming near the sharks is permitted, but not scuba diving. For that, try Baja California Sur or Western Australia's Ningaloo Reef.

White rhinoceros *Ceratotherium simum*

WHAT The largest of the living rhinos is a two tonne lawnmower, with a square lip shaped to maximise grass-cropping efficiency ('white' is derived from the Afrikaans word for 'wide' to describe this feature). While the northern subspecies is functionally extinct, with just three non-breeding individuals surviving under armed guard, numbers of the southern variety are estimated at around 20,000. Income from wildlife tourism is an important factor in combating a drastic recent upsurge in poaching, fuelled by the market for horn used in traditional Chinese medicine, and conservation organisations work closely with many game reserves. **WHERE** The highest densities of white rhino anywhere in the species' range are in the south of South Africa's Kruger National Park, where sightings are pretty much guaranteed in any visit lasting a few days. The Pilanesberg Game Reserve also has a good population, and is accessible in a self-driven daytrip from Johannesburg.

White stork *Ciconia ciconia*

WHAT Large size, conspicuous nesting habits, ardent pair-bonding antics and welcome predation of species which are considered pests by farmers make the white stork a popular species throughout its range. Indeed, pairs returning to chimneys, rooftops and steeples in Alsace, the Black Forest and the Algarve are welcomed as old friends and celebrated in a folk tradition that appeals equally to culture vultures and wildlife tourists. **WHERE** In addition to breeding birds, Portugal's Algarve boasts an end-of-season migration spectacular. In early October, white storks are among the huge numbers of migrants that converge over the Sagres peninsula to take advantage of thermal updrafts that serve as a natural elevator. Several thousand can sometimes be seen spiralling higher and higher, before embarking on a long glide across the neck of the Mediterranean to Africa. Similar spectacles of visible migration can be seen in the Levant.

THE A-Z OF WILDLIFE WATCHING

White-headed duck *Oxyura leucocephala*

WHAT Everyone loves a conservation success story, and the recovery of this delightful stiff-tail duck has earned it celebrity status in much of its range, especially in Spain, where in 1977 the population was thought to be just 22 birds. Today there are around 4500, thanks to protection from hunters, habitat conservation and the controversial culling of introduced American ruddy duck, with which white-heads can interbreed. If your first encounter is with a male, it might not be the white head that strikes you first, but the strange blue bill, like something from a joke shop.

WHERE Spanish white-heads can be seen on natural lakes and abandoned gravel pits in Andalucía's Doñana National Park. But for numbers that seemed impossible a few years ago, your destination should be Kazakhstan, where a recent survey at Korgalzhyn State Nature Reserve confirmed the region as a species stronghold, with an astounding resurgent population of about 20,000 birds today.

Wild boar
Sus scrofa

WHAT While there's nothing pink and porky about this wily forest ancestor of the domestic pig, much of its rather ferocious reputation is exaggerated. In wild areas, sightings are likely to be fleeting as the animals retreat, but they can become bold and inquisitive where contact with humans is frequent or where populations have been boosted by escapees from captivity. The species was extirpated from large parts of its natural range but is expanding once more in many areas, including the UK. Introduced populations also thrive in North America, where they are called wild hogs.

WHERE Boar continue to be relatively abundant in France, and the relatively new National Park of Calanques southeast of Marseille has a strong population, members of which have been known to venture onto busy beaches and suburbia (there are also urban boar in Berlin). Boar are hunted widely, so bright clothing is advisable if you don't want to be mistaken for one.

Wild cat (Scottish) *Felis silvestris grampia*

WHAT The so-called 'Highland Tiger' may look like a domestic tabby, but these feisty felines are as wild as it's possible to be. Their dislike of humans is so intense that long spells of captivity cannot render them tame. This is a challenge for anyone wanting to see one in the wild, but a greater problem is extreme rarity. Recent estimates put the number of pure-bred Scottish wildcats at fewer than 300. Though strictly protected, they are threatened by interbreeding with feral and free-roaming domestic cats. An intensive programme of public education, moggy-neutering and captive breeding is underway. **WHERE** Captive wildcats can be seen in natural enclosures at the Highland Wildlife Park in Kingussie. For a chance of a wild encounter, head to nearby Strathbogie, Strathspey or the Morvern Peninsula. The best chances are in winter when hunger makes them more active.

Wildebeest (brindled gnu) *Connochaetes taurinus*

WHAT If herds of wildebeest sweeping majestically are for you, it's the migrating blue you want, rather than the black variety. Both species are large muscular antelopes, somewhat front-heavy, with long legs. Their gawky geometry belies superb athleticism and agility, which is demonstrated to thrilling effect when fleeing their many predators (lion, cheetah, leopard, crocodile, wild dog, hyenas...) or when travelling en masse between seasonal feeding grounds. They frequently form mixed herds with zebra. **WHERE** Only three populations (the Serengeti and Tarangaire in northern Tanzania and Kafue in Zambia) continue to migrate freely, and of these, the movement between the Southern Serengeti and Kenya's Masai Mara is the biggest, with millions of animals on the move. The most famous spectacle is of vast herds crossing the crocodile-infested waters of the Grumeti and Mara Rivers.

Wobbegong
Eucrossorhinus dasypogon

WHAT Even in well-lit shallow water, the slight bulge of a coral- and algae-encrusted rock at edge of a reef is easily overlooked. For small fish, this is a mistake of the most serious kind. Tasselled wobbegongs are carpet sharks, and masters of camouflage, ambush and deception. They often lie with their back end in a small cave or rock crevice, using gentle movements of the tail to deflect attention from their head and lure curious fish into the shadows. The strike, when it comes, is lightning fast, and relies partly on suction – prey is drawn in on a rush of water entering the huge mouth.

WHERE Wobbegongs are a popular attraction at many dive spots on the northern Great Barrier Reef, especially those on the outer Ribbon Reefs such as Challenger Bay, three hours out from Cairns. The shallow water here is accessible even with snorkelling kit.

Wolverine
Gulo gulo

WHAT A creature of mythic status even before the Marvel comic version, the largest member of the weasel and badger family is a species whose ferocity is matched only by its elusiveness, and perhaps its appetite – though the alternative name 'glutton' is a little unfair; in winter it eats whenever and whatever it can, and large meals are not wasted.

WHERE While a chance encounter with a wolverine will feature high on of any naturalist's list of lifetime highlights, the species' wide-ranging, unpredictable and wary behaviour means the odds are against you. If you're willing to accept a less purist approach, then Finland is the place to go, with many reserves offering chances to see and photograph animals in viewing areas baited with carrion. Some operators boast a 100% success rate at 'secret' locations.

Wombat (common)
Vombatus ursinus

WHAT Barrelling through the undergrowth, a wombat sounds even larger than you'd expect. These stocky mammals grow to a maximum of 1m in length and about half that in height; they're built for burrowing, which they do with great enthusiasm. With their benign nature and cute appearance, they're popular members of Australia's marsupial family and like many of their mates they have some strange habits. For one thing, their poop is square – small, cuboid pellets – and they have a preference for leaving it on a tree stump or rock to alert other wombats to their presence (its shape ensures it won't roll away). So, you'll always know when you're in wombat country.

WHERE Wombats are widely distributed around Australia and even venture into towns and suburbs – look for them grazing at dawn and dusk. For up-close sightings however, Cradle Mountain National Park on Tasmania has some extra relaxed wombats.

Woodchuck *Marmota monax*

WHAT The groundhog or woodchuck is one of 14 species of marmot (large, burrowing members of the squirrel family), but the only one associated with lowland habitats. Its diet of fresh grasses, herbs and fruits is seasonal, so don't bother searching for it in winter – they hibernate for up to six months of the year.

WHERE If you want to join the annual circus of 'Groundhog Day', you need to visit Punxsutawney, Pennsylvania on 2 February, where 140 years of tradition dictate that a celebrity groundhog (known as Phil) will 'predict' the duration of remaining wintry weather. Wild groundhogs can be seen from April to October in reserves, parks and even gardens across a large swathe of North America from Alaska to Nova Scotia and south to Alabama.

Xenopus (African clawed toad) *Xenopus spp*

WHAT These wholly aquatic amphibians lack the flicking tongue used by many other frogs to hunt, and hunt instead by snapping at prey or catching it in their front feet. They are the only frogs with actual claws, which they use to snag and shred food. They will attempt to make a meal of almost anything, using the feet to cram larger items into their mouths. The species is a widely used laboratory animal and sometimes escapes to establish feral populations whose voraciousness can be a menace to native wildlife. **WHERE** Xenopus are native in lakes and rivers across sub-Saharan Africa, where they live quietly, occasionally collected and eaten by people. But introduced populations have become notorious. The San Francisco authorities took drastic measures to eradicate those in Golden Gate Park but feral frogs continue to be cause for concern elsewhere, including 11 US states, and parts of the UK, Germany and the Netherlands. This is one to report if you see it.

Yak (wild) *Bos mutus*

WHAT The wild ancestor of the domestic yak is immense, with some males exceeding 2m at the shoulder and second in stature only to gaur among the surviving wild bovids. Their apparent size is emphasised by a shaggy coat that forms a trailing skirt, resembling the drooping brushes of an inactive automatic carwash. That such bulk can be sustained solely by the grasses and sedges that grow above the Himalayan treeline between 3000m and 5500m seems incredible, but this is where you'll need to go to see them. **WHERE** The vulnerable conservation status and sensitive nature of wild yak makes seeing them a somewhat specialist occupation, but if you're determined, Changtang National Nature Reserve in Tibet is home to some 7000 animals, about half the world population. Domesticated yak (*Bos grunniens*), on the other hand, can be seen easily throughout the Himalayan region.

Zebra *Equus quagga*

WHAT Plains zebras are the smallest of the three zebra species, but also the most numerous. They are prodigious grazers, and play an important pioneering role, creating the short grass conditions needed by more selective feeders such as antelope. Those iconic and individually unique coats probably serve in social recognition as well as potentially confusing predators during a chase. **WHERE** Zebra herds come as standard in the extensive parks of southern and eastern Africa including Kruger, Serengeti, Okavango and Chobe. Often the best action is to be had at watering holes, with those in drier landscapes such as Namibia's Etosha National Park being most reliable. Makgadikgadi Pan in Botswana sees vast numbers of zebra arriving after annual rains, accompanied by similarly numerous wildebeest.

© Kerrin | 500px

Zorilla *Ictonyx striatus*

WHAT This attractive-looking mustelid is also known as the African skunk – and the similarity doesn't end at its striking black and white livery. When threatened, it turns away, but instead of fleeing, raises its tail like a bottlebrush, ready to squirt a dose of predator-repelling stink sufficiently potent to temporarily blind an inquisitive lion. While effective on most mammals, this defence has no effect on vehicles and hence the species is most often seen as roadkill.

WHERE Zorillas are widespread in grassland and scrub areas of Africa south of the Sahara, such as South Africa's Tankwa Karoo National Park. They are active after dark, and mostly likely to be spotted by their eyeshine – the beam of a torch or car headlights reflected in their dark-adapted eyes.

Index

Index

The A-Z of Wildlife Watching
September 2018
Published by Lonely Planet Global Limited
ISBN 9781787014312
CRN 554153
www.lonelyplanet.com
10 9 8 7 6 5 4 3 2 1
Printed in China
© Lonely Planet 2018
© Photographers as indicated 2018

Managing Director, Publishing Piers Pickard
Associate Publisher & Commissioning Editor Robin Barton
Art Director & Design Daniel Di Paolo
Author Amy-Jane Beer
Editor Yolanda Zappatera
Picture Research Regina Wolek
Cover photos Jonathan Gregson (main images);
small images by (L-R) Peter Grunert, Matt Munro,
Philip Lee Harvey, Catherine Sunderland
Print Production Lisa Ford, Nigel Longuet
Thanks Tina Garcia

Australia
The Malt Store, Level 3,
551 Swanston St, Carlton, Victoria 3053
T: 03 8379 8000

USA
124 Linden St, Oakland,
CA 94607
T: 510 250 6400

Ireland
Digital Depot, Roe Lane (off Thomas St),
Digital Hub, Dublin 8 D08 TCV4

Europe
240 Blackfriars Rd,
London SE1 8NW
T: 020 3771 5100

STAY IN TOUCH: lonelyplanet.com/contact